My Dear Alex

Letters from the KGB

MY DEAR
Alex

LETTERS FROM
THE KGB

Dinesh D'Souza
and Gregory Fossedal

REGNERY GATEWAY

LIBRARY OF CONGRESS CATALOGING-IN-PUBLICATION DATA

D'Souza, Dinesh, 1961–
  My dear Alex.
  I. Fossedal, Gregory A. II. Title.
PR9499.3.D76M9 1987   823   87-9720
ISBN 0-89526-576-1

Published in the United States by
Regnery Gateway
1130 17th Streeet, NW
Washington, DC 20036

Distributed to the trade by
Kampmann & Company, Inc.
9 E. 40th Street
New York, NY 10016

10 9 8 7 6 5 4 3 2 1

Foreword

My Dear Alex is an important and unique book that makes deadly serious points in a delightfully clever way. It traces the exploits of Vladimir, a seasoned Soviet propaganda specialist and star guest on such shows as "Nightline" and "Phil Donahue," and Alex, his young protégé recently arrived in the United States after a successful internship at *Pravda*. Their mission: to undermine the domestic unity and foreign policy of the United States during President Reagan's first term.

Whether they are gleaning the columns of *The Washington Post* for good arguments against the Strategic Defense Initiative, showing up at a Hollywood fundraising party for the Soviet-backed Sandinista communists, or clipping an editorial from *National Review* that argues against putting economic pressure on the Soviet Union, Alex and Vladimir are always up to something interesting—something that illuminates both what the Soviets are up to in the world and, equally vital, how we as a society cope with them. The book is an enjoyable read—such as when Alex, shortly after his arrival in America, must carry around a chart showing how to string together various meaningless buzzwords for smart-set cocktail parties: "mutual interpersonal oneness," "complex meaningful dialogues," "compassionate interactive reality," and so on. But *My Dear Alex* is also serious in the best sense of the word.

To be effective, a satire must be more than funny. First,

it must bear some resemblance to reality, and this book does. One remarkable development in recent years is the emergence of a suave new brand of Soviet spokesmen who more or less openly intervene in Western politics. The struggle between the United States and the Soviet Union is largely a war of ideas, and the Kremlin has shown increasing sophistication in its propaganda—adopting Western idiom to attack Western governments and prompting the rise of figures remarkably similar to Vladimir in *My Dear Alex*.

There are those, in fact, who may find this novel's proximity to reality too close for comfort. When Vladimir or Alex cites a prominent U.S. politician or journalist arguing for the Soviet position, authors Fossedal and D'Souza are quoting from an actual speech, book, or article. The names have *not* been changed to protect the guilty. No doubt this will infuriate some of the people named—another characteristic of good satire. A close reading of the book, however, shows that the authors are not out to impugn individuals. In fact, they pointedly defend the motives of their opponents. Only statements and positions are made to look ridiculous, and if the people who made them *feel* ridiculous after rereading them, that's a matter for them to explain.

Indeed, one encouraging characteristic of the United States in the last 25 years is that virtually no one explicitly defends the Soviet system, its aims, or the ideology underlying it. No one with a serious voice claims any more, as Nikita Khrushchev did in his "kitchen debate" with me in 1959, that communism will "bury" the democracies. No one of note defends the aims of the Soviet Union. And yet, as Vladimir notes, many in the West wind up defending the Soviet Union's stand on issue after issue. Why? D'Souza and Fossedal, it seems to me, have some plausible but worrisome explanations. Yet they also demonstrate ecumenism in poking fun at their own views and those of their heroes. William Buckley and the hawkish editorials of *The Wall Street Journal* (Fossedal's own former bailiwick) come in for a needle just as surely as do Ted Kennedy, Anthony Lewis, and the dovish editorials of *The New York Times*. And that is a final mark of good satire, indeed of all good writing: fairness. I don't agree with everything that Fossedal and D'Souza, through the letters of Vladimir, have to say. But I applaud them for saying it with economy, wit, and a commendable sympathy for their targets.

The West has needed a book like this for some time. Not since George Orwell, to my knowledge, has there been a broad political satire to match *My Dear Alex*. That's a shame, because as Fossedal and D'Souza show, laughter may be one of the most effective weapons in the arsenal of democracy. It is also good medicine for many of the maladies of our own society—among them a tendency on the part of people on all sides of the debate to take themselves too seriously.

My Dear Alex achieves what Swift described as the highest goal of satire: pointing "a sort of mirror" on ourselves. This book not only affords reading pleasure; it illuminates and provokes. It should command a wide audience and serious critical attention.

—Richard M. Nixon

My Dear Alex

Letters From a KGB Agent

My dear Alex:

Thank you for your complimentary letter—and so soon after your arrival in the United States. Our superiors are well aware of the dangerous situation that is developing here. A man of tremendous hostility to our government has been elected President, and by a landslide. His party platform promises to work for "military superiority" over the Soviet Union. You and I know that this is an extremely unrealistic goal, especially over a short span of four years. Yet our country has invested a great deal of time and money in trying to ensure that such a goal would not even be *desired*, much less actively pursued, by Americans. Ronald Reagan's statements suggest an unfortunate alertness to the advances of Communism. If Congress consistently supports Reagan's proposals for defense increases, our foreign policy objectives will suffer a setback. Moscow has sent you to America to help prevent that.

Congratulations on your outstanding performance at the Lenin School. We need men of your caliber to help defeat the adversary. Fortunately, this adversary is divided and rather naive, and we have many allies in powerful places. So we are likely to win, after all. But we cannot win immediately, and we cannot win simply by marshalling our formidable military forces. We have to rely on corrosion within the body of the enemy.

How do we help produce this? Much as I regret to begin on this note, I must urge you to forget most of the lessons you so dutifully absorbed in your propaganda classes and your editorial internship at *Pravda*. America is a very different country from ours. Its people operate on somewhat different assumptions. We must take this into account in our work. Remember that we are in this country for purposes of *practical* propaganda. This goal is not well served by using methods such as those developed by the KGB, effective though they may be at home.

In your introductory letter, you express confusion over why the American people would elect what you call a "self-proclaimed fascist" such as Ronald Reagan to their highest office. Let me be candid. I share your strong feelings about Reagan, yet I do not recommend that you use such language in public. Because Reagan comes across as personable and warm, no serious criticism of him is possible which does not take this into account. Make a snide remark about how Reagan's virtues are "artificial," and allude to his Hollywood background. Then shift the focus from the man to his policies. Insist that the American people didn't vote *for* Ronald Reagan, they voted *against* Jimmy Carter (voting is a popular American custom; no doubt you have read up on this already) so Reagan does not have a mandate for his policies.

We must help defeat Reagan at the hands of his own people. Your amateur suggestion that we work out a way to assassinate the President I find most implausible, indeed laughable. No, Alex, we must use the four years we have to generate deep divisions among the American people, and to encourage hatred for Reagan's policies among the intelligentsia. Curiously, the best tactics for doing this have been developed by Americans, not by us. I suggest you begin reading the works of Michael Harrington, Mary McGrory, Arthur Schlesinger, John Kenneth Galbraith, Garry Wills, and Lester Thurow. Anthony Lewis of *The New York Times* is absolutely indispensable. I'm also sending along some of my recent op-ed articles to give you an idea of desirable approaches to undermining America's economic system and her will to defend herself.

Sincerely yours,

Vladimir

My dear Alex:

You should have checked with me before attending a cocktail party so shortly after your arrival. I understand that the left-wing Institute for Policy Studies (IPS) wanted you to "meet the boys," as you put it. But from your account, you have managed to make a fool of yourself, as I would have expected.

You say you could barely understand the conversation. Even the IPS founders, Richard Barnet and Marcus Raskin, who seemed sympathetic, were talking a "different language, certainly not the language of Lenin," you say. Of course they don't talk in those terms, Alex. That is simply not acceptable conversation in America. Even our Marxist friends operate in disguise, just as it is going to be necessary for you, yes you, to make your conversation indistinguishable from theirs.

Haven't you read my columns? Notice that I do not identify myself as a Communist; in fact, I always go out of my way to say that I "reject labels. They don't mean much anymore." I am quoted in a *Boston Globe* profile denouncing the "saber rattling policies of the new Reagan administration." In my piece on abortion I note that "there are no easy answers to complex questions." In other columns, you will find references to the "decaying infrastructure," "the tensions necessary to the life of the church," "rolling back the civil rights gains of the sixties," and "pluralistic context."

You probably wonder what all this means. Answer: not much, really. Oddly enough, the best way to make your case in this country is often to say things that sound profound but mean little or nothing. This is not for the reason you may suspect: that Americans are generally a stupid people, and inhospitable to clear-minded arguments. In fact, the opposite is true. Americans are generally very good at making intelligent choices when faced with concrete options. They are adept at weighing advantages and disadvantages. This is precisely why we need a language such as that developed by our allies on the American left, a language that confounds the issues and carpets them with banalities and pseudo-profound references.

To italicize differences between capitalism and socialism, or between America and the Soviet Union, would invite people to choose. Our goal is to convey the impression that there *are* no important differences between the two economic and political systems. We want to make socialism seem unthreatening, so that we can coax America in that direction without its citizens ever knowing it, or being alarmed. If some shrewd observer notices the differences between us and them, everybody around him will laugh and assure him that he is being paranoid.

When you are fluent in the language I want you to learn, you will no longer speak as a Soviet spokesman but as a "specialist in Soviet-American relations." That is how American intellectuals will treat you. You will feel comfortable in their circles, and enjoy all the prestige and credibility that the American people attach to their "experts." Our strategy, Alex, is to become part of the Western intelligentsia and see that it continues to serve our interests. The American people will, I hope, follow their educated elites.

I don't know your aptitude for new languages, so I have prepared a game, which I call "Feelings," to help you master the vocabulary of American liberalism. Take a look at the three columns below:

COLUMN X	COLUMN Y	COLUMN Z
Profound	*Interpersonal*	*Awareness*
Diverse	*Emotional*	*Oneness*
Genuine	*Dialectical*	*Relationship*
Subjective	*Harmonious*	*Network*
Complex	*Communal*	*Correspondence*

6

Sophisticated	*Open*	*Linkage*
Realistic	*Humane*	*Consensus*
Meaningful	*Interactive*	*Context*
Mutual	*Collective*	*Dialogue*
Objective	*Societal*	*Forum*

Alex, you are to pick one word from each of the three columns and string them together in a phrase. Thus you can have a "profound, dialectical relationship," or a "meaningful, societal oneness," or a "genuine, interactive linkage," or a "sophisticated, humane consensus." See how it works? Keep this as a handy reference for future encounters with American intellectuals.

Sincerely yours,

Vladimir

My dear Alex:

Disturbing reports are beginning to pile up on my desk about your performance at Norman Lear's reception, and today is only Tuesday. How many more letters will arrive to describe your clumsy behavior? First you have problems with the language, and now these social blunders. I hope I don't have to continue to give you belated advice when the damage is already done.

Alex, I will admit that, as they were described to me, the *hors d'oeuvres* were excessive. Even Politburo members do not usually enjoy such a high grade of caviar. I can understand your revulsion at such a display of decadence; indeed, the fault was partly mine for suggesting you go before you were properly briefed. Even so, you had no call to hurl your wine glass onto the floor and launch into a diatribe on "the starving infants of Africa and India." If some of the guests snickered, it is because such horror stories are already considered cliche in America.

You may think it a contradiction for guests to worry about "the victims of Reaganomics" while sipping expensive champagne in a Manhattan townhouse. But I assure you, Americans have already accepted and internalized many such contradictions. Ted Kennedy blasts tuition tax credits, but sends his children to the best private schools. Ronald Reagan vaunts religious and family values, yet he goes to church less than four times a year. You will get nowhere here if you are going to be an anti-social pest. Keep your standards so high and you will spend four years talking to no one but that columnist at *The Nation*, Alex Cockburn. I only hope that Norm accepts my letter of explanation.

Your general attitude towards American affluence should be one of meekness and awe. A good conversation starter at the party, for example, would be, "I must admit, the American economic system has produced some tremendous wonders. I have travelled far, yet I have never seen such an abundance of material things." This suggests that the system produces *merely* things, heaps of tinsel and garbage; but if your guest is a bit slow to catch this implication you might mention some specifics, such as fatuous television advertising.

In one of my better moments, I once turned to Jane Fonda and said, "Jane, let us be fair. America produces more than half of the world's automobiles, with less than five percent of the world's people. On the other hand, America also consumes more than two-thirds of the world's energy, also with the same small share of people. It all balances out." When she recovered from her initial guilt, she launched into a long diatribe against multinational corporations and materialistic culture and "the worship of profits." Marvelous, *n'est-ce pas?*

Alex, I know it goes against your training to make any such admissions to the West, but you will find it is much more effective to confess what is clearly true. The key is to twist that truth to our advantage, and not to get caught up in hopeless arguments to the effect that capitalism is "doomed to crumble."

Sincerely yours,

Vladimir

9

April 1981

My dear Alex:

Ronald Reagan is about to present his tax and budget proposals to Congress. He seems likely to get his way. I don't know if we should even fight this one; it is infinitely more important to concentrate on his military proposals.

Perhaps you should write a few essays on economic policy aimed at long-lasting impressions, though. The first piece you sent me on the subject is woefully inadequate; in fact, I hardly know where to begin my criticisms.

You write that "The final victory of socialism is guaranteed by the internal contradictions within the capitalist system. Only the socialist system of production can provide social justice for all men." You also remark that "The Communist Party, with its scientific grasp of history, can alone lead the people to prosperity and the world to peace and justice for all."

It is hard to do much worse than this. Socialism is a discredited philosophy in America, although it has a following in some top universities. So let people have the idea of socialism without the formal trimmings, and certainly without the label.

Please rewrite your column to stress the fact that "there are two Americas, one for the rich and one for the poor." For many, the American dream is "a cruel hoax." You may wonder a bit about this, Alex. One of the inconveniences of this argument is that most of the wealth in America is concentrated in the middle class. Yet we should highlight the distance between the richest and poorest people in America, ignoring the middle class. The purpose of this is to provoke the strong egalitarian sense in the American people, what Tocqueville called their "smoldering hatred" of elitism. Also we want to foment violent envy against those Americans who are rich, to heighten political pressure for government to take away their resources and distribute them to the proletariat.

I am completely enthralled by the liberal argument which maintains, in effect, that there is nothing in principle right or wrong with socialism, but somehow it's always the right thing to do at any given time. Consider poverty programs, for example. When the economy is in good shape, then "it is all the more shameful that some must live in squalor," and the country "must be generous with our less privileged brethren . . . there is no excuse for being stingy now." If, on the other hand, America is in a recession, then "these programs are needed today more than ever . . . this is no time to shred the safety net," etc. Add the two together and you see that for the American left, it is *always* the right time for redistribution.

Don't bother to refute supply-side economics. Simply call it a "theology" which is "pretty simplistic." Other reliable lines opposing Reagan's free market proposals are "The problem with capitalism is that it has never been tried" and "We live in an international marketplace now. The old solutions don't work."

I look forward to seeing your revised draft in print.

Sincerely yours,

Vladimir

May 1981

My dear Alex:

I meant to answer your letter sooner, but the attempt on Reagan's life has had me very depressed. I don't just mean that we have now lost several months hard work building up the image of him as a villain, though this is not a negligible consideration. No, frankly, I'm afraid this is going to haunt us for some time.

There is some consolation in the fact that we were not involved in this one. Still, in terms of the implications for American politics, this incident will cast a deep and indelible impression on the American psyche of Reagan as the immortal hero, a man who can grin with a bullet in his chest. We won't be able to use the "cowboy" or "former movie actor" rhetoric for some time to come; Reagan's performance has rendered those terms comically ineffective, almost counterproductive really, calling to mind the very attributes we want people to forget.

At least your reaction shows some sophistication. That's something to be thankful for. I agree that there are some limited opportunities in it for our friends. Everyone who will be bashing Reagan's defense plans or economic policy six weeks from now can write their pious patriotism piece this week before getting back to work on the real agenda. Still, I don't know if I have the stomach to sit through another one of these spectacles. It gets bad enough on the Fourth of July.

Anyway, you'll forgive me if I cut this off. The way things are going, somebody will probably take a shot at the Pope and miss too. It is too disheartening to even think about.

Sincerely yours,

Vladimir

My dear Alex:

Well, we lost on Reagan's tax and budget proposals, didn't we? I wouldn't fret too much. It was anticipated. The American intelligentsia was simply too listless to pose any serious opposition. They really need a waiting period, I feel. In fact, I find myself in the curious position of reassuring these people when they come to me apologizing for their ineffectiveness.

I notice your vocabulary is improving, as well as your sources. You quoted both Jonathan Schell and Tom Wicker in your last piece. Not a single reference to *Pravda*. Excellent. You also managed to use the terms "global thermonuclear holocaust," "abject, grinding poverty," and "Cold War paranoia" in the same sentence. You are now working on systematizing all this jargon, which is very good.

One hint I would offer: stop using all words that end in "ist," such as "imperialist," "monopolist," "colonialist," or "fascist." Remember that these words suggest concrete systems which, your reader will easily verify, have little to do with American policies. And even if they do, the reader will be able to weigh these systems against competing ones. We don't want to encourage any such comparisons. So use "tic" words, which all convey feelings and tendencies rather than facts. I recommend "unrealistic," "simplistic," "opportunistic," "militaristic," and "pragmatic."

As I say, your language is better, but your arguments still cause me some embarrassment. In the draft of your speech scheduled for the Union of Concerned Scientists meeting next week you blame "American imperialism" for the problems of the world. You say the Soviet Union is much stronger than the U.S. and would pulverize her in a showdown. In an attempt to explain our presence in Afghanistan, you use that old line about being "invited to resist CIA incursions from

Pakistan, and to curtail corruption and repression of human rights."

This convinces me that you need a solid theoretical grounding in the arguments you should use while in the U.S. I think the problem lies with your preconceived notions of the U.S. and your ideological over-enthusiasm. Let me explain.

Never say that the Soviet Union is a Marxist society. You know that it is really not and are surprised, perhaps, at my suggestion that you tell the truth. But sometimes it is fact, not propaganda, which is most effective. Here is a formulation you should strive for. I quote from Roger Molander, founder of the Ground Zero anti-nuclear organization: "Marxism-Leninism has undoubtedly had some impact on Soviet policy, but it is important to emphasize the danger of confusing Marxist-Leninist doctrine with the beliefs, or mindset, of the Soviet people and policymakers. The Soviet leaders and the average Soviet citizen are no longer much moved by ideological cant— by the ritualized allusions to Marxism-Leninism."

But you must immediately go on to add Molander's next statement: "But this is far from the same as their being without perspectives on the world, perspectives that are vastly different from ours." The reason for this addition is that while you want to allay fears that our country operates on a philosophy that Americans dislike, you want to put enough distance between the American and Soviet temperament so that future Soviet attacks can be attributed not to ruthless power-hunger but to cultural differences between the two nations.

For example, Alex, hard as it is for you to understand, you must insist that our Soviet leaders are frightened fellows, haunted by memories of World War II and eternally worried that their borders will be savaged by next-door countries. George Kennan, the American diplomat, has some wonderful stuff on this. He describes our leaders as possessed by "a congenital sense of insecurity," and a "neurotic fear of penetration." They are "easily frightened" and, in Kennan's words, frustrated, secretive, defensive, troubled, and anxious.

The advantages of this characterization are obvious. First, it suggests that these are Soviet attitudes to be humored. Any and all U.S. arms can be seen to destabilize the world by irresponsibly whipping up Soviet paranoia. Also, all our country's invasions of small countries can be explained as expressions of this tiresome but understandable cultural quirk.

Be careful not to make our leaders' paranoia a regular feature of the Russian temperament, though. If it is, how can you expect Americans to place faith in rational negotiations with our leaders? Nobody wants to deal with neurotic and paranoid cranks. The Americans should worry about feeding the paranoia of our leaders, but they should get a general impression of them as otherwise sober, stable, conservative, and cautious.

In your speech, you refer to "myths about Soviet atrocities spread by right-wing propaganda." I like the bit about right-wing propaganda, Alex, but I think the term "McCarthyism" would be more suitable here. The connotations surrounding that term are one of our major rhetorical victories of the last several decades. Your attempt to decry "myths about Soviet atrocities" won't go anywhere though. I suggest you argue along the "Of course, but" line, i.e. "Of course the Soviet Union is not a perfect society, and of course it has made its share of mistakes, but so has the U.S." (This is a good time to mention slavery.) "Therefore, it is fruitless to make comparisons that are sure to feed Cold War paranoia." You may also note that we live in a nuclear age when the U.S. and the Soviet Union together "have enough nuclear weapons to destroy every city of any size in the world 10 times over."

Finally, I have discovered in George Kennan's writing an artful way to diminish American fears of our leaders: wildly exaggerate them. As Kennan puts it, "The Soviet leaders appear (in the view of conservatives) as a terrible and forbidding group of men: monsters of sorts . . . men who have all internal problems essentially solved and (are) therefore free to spend their time evolving elaborate schemes for some ultimate military showdown—men who are prepared to accept the most tremendous risks, and to place upon their people the most fearful sacrifices, if only in this way their program of destruction or domination of ourselves and our allies can be carried forward." By setting up this straw man view of Soviet leaders, Alex, you don't even have to attack it; it falls down by itself.

Sincerely yours,

Vladimir

My dear Alex:

Here are some strategies you should employ in your up-coming "Nightline" debate with Bill Buckley on Reagan's foreign policy.

1. THE "WHOM DOES THE U.S. HAVE TO FEAR?" AP-PROACH: This is very devious because it seems flattering to your American listener. Argue that the U.S. is the most powerful nation on earth with the largest industrial base and the most advanced technology. Say that the U.S. has a literate and well-fed citizenry, a talented labor force, and a creative intellectual elite. The American people live on a rich continent with long but safe borders. Whom do American leaders have to fear? Certainly not the Soviet Union. Yet they still seem to be "running scared" of Moscow. The purpose of this argument is to imply that our country does not pose a threat worth worrying about.

2. THE "COMMUNISM ISN'T THE REAL ENEMY" AP-PROACH: Poverty and social injustice are. The right wing "confuses nationalism with Communism." You know this argument. The U.S. should ally itself with the forces of liberation, i.e., help countries go Communist. To pursue any other course is to "drive these Third World countries into the arms of the Soviets." I have a juicy addition to this point. Note the irony that "President Reagan claims that Communism is the real enemy, but he doesn't seem to find anything wrong with Communist China. There are now good Communists and bad Communists. The Chinese, for the moment, are good Communists."

3. THE "SMILE KNOWINGLY AND CONDESCENDINGLY" PLOY: This is not an argument, but it avoids your having to make one. If Buckley ever mentions a "Communist plot" or repeats President Reagan's statement that Soviet Communism is "the focus of evil in the modern world"—don't attempt to refute this. Just throw up your hands and smile knowingly. "There you go again" should be conveyed by your facial expression. The idea is to subtly mock such statements, to make claims like that seem terribly unsophisticated, to get people to laugh when they are repeated.

4. THE "WHO'S THE REAL AGGRESSOR?" ARGUMENT: Alex, you are not to present Ronald Reagan as the sole enemy of peace in the world. Rather, you are to suggest that he is contributing to the international tensions which make nuclear war more likely. Say: "The Pentagon talks endlessly about war and prepares actively for war. Generals plan for a nuclear war. Even Vice President Bush spoke about a *limited* nuclear war." This inevitably brings gasps from the audience. I am not sure why any use of nuclear weapons necessarily leads to an all-out exchange in which the whole world is blown up, but disarmament groups have done a good job spreading that idea and we should not debunk it. Conclude this argument by saying in a hushed tone, "What Reagan really wants is overwhelming military supremacy over the Soviet Union." Pause dramatically. Wait for applause. (It will come, Alex. I know *our* people cheer when they are told we have military supremacy, but in the U.S. this is regarded, by some people at least, as a bad thing.)

5. THE "GESTURES OF GOODWILL" PLEA: The point here is that you call for overtures which lead to more overtures *ad infinitum*. Why not suggest that the U.S. should

extend diplomatic recognition, the opening up of trade and tourism, and the potential for private investment to Cuba? When Buckley points out Castro's more disagreeable qualities, simply argue that "very little is lost by minor concessions that can easily be reversed if Castro is not receptive." The actual approach is never to allow any reversals on the ground that they would "send the wrong signals" to Castro. So even if Castro continued to bankroll the revolution in Central America, as we will surely insist he does, Americans will continue to ignore his efforts in the continuing hope that he will someday be more "reasonable" toward them.

Good luck in the debate. Take a dictionary along; Buckley is disposed to be polysyllabic, especially when he is losing the argument.

Sincerely yours,

Vladimir

December 1981

My dear Alex:

Your letter to the Politburo urging "real action against the counter-revolution in Poland" shows you still have much strategy to learn. Frankly, the party is handling the situation there as best it can, rather skillfully in fact. Solidarity has been effectively checked without an invasion and hardly any violence, a great tactical success.

Even so, the coming months will be a time of great danger. You worry that our crackdown is not harsh enough, failing to make a sufficient example for the East Germans. I worry that, subtle though the policy has been, it will still tend to unify and strengthen the West. You are about to witness one of those rare outbreaks of serious thinking about Soviet objectives I have warned you about. Everything about the situation is wrong: the large Polish and Catholic presence here, along with such groups as the Jews who understand the Polish complaint; the natural union sympathies; and of course, the popularity of the Pope. I tell you that for a few weeks, even Max Frankel at *The New York Times* will be supporting U.S. policy. (Just you wait and see.)

Because you are used to seeing only the great divisions which democracy tolerates, you no doubt find it hard to conceive of the spontaneous unity it can occasionally generate. There will be picnics, marches, candlelight vigils, and even football half time shows—all devoted, not to disarming the U.S., but to opposing the Soviet Union. In such a mood, with that nauseating, peculiarly American combination of joy and resolve so prevalent, I tell you that the West is capable of almost anything.

Fortunately, we have done quite a bit of groundwork to prevent any resolute action. Consider, if you will, the following excerpts from a recent editorial in *The New York Times:*

The first obligation, to the Poles and to ourselves, is to admit the truth. The Soviet fist in Eastern Europe remains mightier than Western words or sanctions. If there is a combination of domestic upheaval and Western pressure that can promote democracy there, it remains to be discovered . . .

The bitter news from Poland is that General Jaruzelski has beaten Solidarity . . .

So the aims and the means of Western policy toward the Soviet Union need urgent attention. Military power is obviously unusable . . . How then can economic power and diplomacy be used constructively? . . . The real failure in Poland is not, after all, that of the West. It is the Communist system that failed. It survives by force, but it will not flourish or make the Soviet Union secure until it is allowed to evolve . . .

How to promote that evolution? . . . It implies an effort to recostruct detente . . . It implies effective arms control and also agreed norms of conduct for the superpower rivalry around the globe . . .

You see? Much of the American elite has actually convinced itself there is *nothing* that can be done about the expansion of Soviet power. Part of this has to do with mere sloppy thinking, because the same people who decry the fruitlessness of an embargo against us will rush to urge one against South Africa.

Another reason for the Western inertia is "the lessons of Vietnam." I was not here at the time, but it seems the Americans went in convinced they could solve every problem in the world, from poverty to overpopulation to water pollution. When their will to fight collapsed and the puppet Thieu was overrun by our allies, America's leaders convinced themselves that the U.S. could accomplish nothing at all. If you don't believe me, just mention any of the following phrases to any educated American and observe the talismanic effect: 1. the "limits of power," 2. the "discredited domino theory," 3. the "simplistic fear of a monolithic world Communism," and, if pressed into a corner, 4. the "idealistic notion that America can act as the world's policeman."

People in the West also tend to believe that we live in an especially dangerous time—"nuclear age" is the phrase most often used—which rules out almost any concrete action by the U.S. to undermine Communism. Again, the reasoning is a bit obscure, but in practice it means that if we are shipping arms to Nicaragua, the Americans try to stop us, and we start a nuclear war, then it would be America's fault. "Escalation" is a key word here, along with "the ultimate conflict." Obviously, this is not the exact idea, because we are never accused of pushing *Reagan* towards war, not even by the Europeans. But you get the gist.

Alex, our greatest ally in a situation like this is time. If you strum one theme in your "Today" show appearance with Bryant Gumbel, strum this: that whatever America does, it must not over-react; that the chance for miscalculation is too great; that this is no time to be hasty (conditions in Poland are admittedly tense, but will not be improved by harsh rhetoric); that a great power must act with restraint.

In other words, delay, delay, delay—and then, delay. Every day the Americans do nothing we are a bit safer. The test of your efforts and mine will be if, one morning a year or two from now, we wake up and realize that we have not thought about Poland for months—because we, like the West, had forgotten.

Sincerely yours,

Vladimir

My dear Alex:

For once, your analysis hits the nail on the head. While the Americans have, thank God, done nothing militarily, the announced policy of sanctions is indeed serious. Moscow can ill afford to lose the gas pipeline to Europe now. I am having our international lawyers work up a brief showing that Reagan has no right to control technology and credit licenses being transferred to us by the West Germans and the Swedes.

And yet, precisely because the policy is serious, we cannot afford to say so. That is why your suggestion for a piece arguing this is all "discreet warfare" and "could seriously impair the START talks" does not quite hit the mark. Others will make these arguments later, when it is more appropriate. For now, our prime task is to convince Americans that the sanctions, or any future actions, *won't work*. Here are some detailed responses to any particular courses of action that might be recommended in the coming weeks. Keep it on file; these are usable in almost any situation.

Economic Sanctions   The market will thwart them. Only work if all U.S. allies cooperate. Hurt our industry, farmers, and foreign exchange just as much as they do theirs. (Alex, make sure to quote free trade editorials from *The Wall Street Journal* or *National Review* here. The right is much more credible than the left on the subject of fighting Communism, and when we can ally with the right, this is an ideal situation.)

Covert Action   Gets found out anyway. Use words like "not so secret" and "so-called clandestine" to describe it. Alienates other countries, driving them into the arms of Communism. Alex, here you give our American allies credibility by saying something like, "Those of us from the Soviet Union wish to thank President Reagan for using the CIA to harass private citizens in other countries, thus helping my government to win new friends and solidify old alliances."

Military Force Should be used only if—a) requested by all the countries involved; b) done in accordance with international law (as interpreted by the World Court); c) used in moderation to avoid chances of embroiling the country in an escalating conflict; d) needed to protect a vital interest; e) approved beforehand in thorough consultation with the NATO allies, Israel, Latin neighbors to the south, Japan, the House and Senate; and f) applied only when all efforts at a negotiated settlement have failed. Threatens to become another Vietnam.

Military Aid to U.S. Allies Tends to go to corrupt right-wing dictators who trample on human rights. Makes America an "arms merchant," thus fueling the "military industrial complex." Threatens to involve American ground forces. Fails to solve the "root problems" that "make revolution inevitable." Winds up going mostly to the guerrillas anyway. Cannot be justified until there is "hard evidence" the Soviets are shipping arms to the rebels. Cannot stem the tide of change. The corrupt government must fall sometime. Sounds suspiciously like the Nixon rationale for aid to Vietnam.

Military Aid to Insurgents A drastic violation of international law. Makes the U.S. a terrorist nation. Not unlike the policy of Libya or the P.L.O. which the President criticizes. Cannot establish a tide of change; the government, while corrupt and imperfect, appears stable. So-called freedom fighters are mostly right-wing members of the former military regime. May wind up hurting the rebels, tarring them with an "American puppet" image. Most of the weapons wind up being seized by the government, anyway. Could be a reverse-Vietnam for the United States.

Economic Aid   Justified, but must be for humanitarian, not political purposes. Should go to countries that are making progress in terms of social justice: raising taxes, devaluing the currency, failing to pay off debt, etc. Unfortunately, much tends to get siphoned off by wealthy right-wing landowners; therefore, land reform is also necessary. Above all, should not be used to force a U.S.-style democracy on the recipient country. Cannot work if countries refuse to displace the oligarchy, as in Vietnam.

Voice of America Broadcasts   Megaphone diplomacy. Tends to spew out Western propaganda. Only angers the Soviet government and holds out false hope to the people.

Whatever you say, Alex, never fail to bring up the "moral high ground." Americans seem to think one loses it every time one pursues any policy other than appeasement.

Sincerely yours,

Vladimir

My dear Alex:

Things are going well. The economy has dropped into what promises to be a deep recession. But this is no time to be smug. If we can spread the notion that the recession was deliberately introduced to make the poor and the unemployed bear the brunt of Reagan's failed policies, so much the better.

Our emphasis, however, continues to be on foreign policy. And I simply don't understand your reservations about the nuclear freeze movement. By now, you should be able to distinguish the ritualistic cant of American political movements from their true objectives.

You want to know why the freeze pamphlets continually stress that only a "mutual" halt to nuclear production is contemplated. You worry that the qualification that an agreement must be "verifiable" will render the movement completely useless. I must say, you were are not at your best when you wrote that, Alex. Thank goodness the freeze advocates are not using your method. The nuclear freeze proposal, neatly timed to coincide with Reagan's plans to increase military spending, is a potentially momentous development for us. If this idea goes through, surely those dangerous Pershing and Cruise missiles will never be deployed in Europe. If that happens, your entire salary will be justified a thousand times over (although right now I am beginning to wonder why we're paying you and not Tony Lewis: did you see his fantastic piece whooping up the freeze?).

The beauty of the freeze movement, as we have seen in the early Vermont town meetings and city rallies, is that it has wide appeal. Didn't you see all the housewives and blue-collar workers at the New York rally? *The New York Times* did. Clearly there is something interesting and useful going on here. The freeze organizers do not demand one-sided arms reductions because then they would immediately lose the support of their soft constituency, the people who don't particularly want to be blown up but are still very suspicious of our intentions. Let the activists exert their bland, generalized pressure for arms talks and mutual restraint. We'll ensure that those impressionistic sentiments are put to use in concrete, beneficial ways.

I also understand that Reagan is planning to deploy the MX missile, the B-1 bomber, and an expanded fleet of Trident submarines. I suggest you spend some time studying each of them; you should be able to look up some rather detailed articles on their design and characteristics in any general American library. (I'm serious. You can. I will explain this later.) Memorize in particular how much each will cost, what its many flaws are, and which U.S. politicians say it is not in the American interest to build it.

You are right to be skeptical of the benefits of any particular political movement in the West, even the freeze, but you must not get so bogged down in theorizing that you neglect your job. Our business is to make all these movements work in our favor. We will see what it all means later on.

Sincerely yours,

Vladimir

May 1982

My dear Alex:

Just a short note to express my satisfaction over your magazine series on social issues. How very timely it was, coming right after President Reagan's speech supporting the Human Life Amendment and voluntary school prayer. I noted with delight your remark "Who is to say when life begins?" and was positively ecstatic over your ironic observation that "the so-called prolifers favor the death penalty." School prayer, you wisely noted, "threatens the wall of separation between church and state that the American founders were so keen to maintain." Enclosed is a note from Arthur Schlesinger, Jr. praising your "thoughtful and deeply moving" presentation. Good work, comrade.

Sincerely yours,

Vladimir

P.S. Understandably, you are baffled by the concept of busing; perhaps the closest thing we have to this at home is sending people to Siberia. You shrewdly recognize the parallels between busing and our country's practice of separating children from their homes. But then you go on to suggest that this American program may be "a bizarre compromise" by which children are allowed to stay with their parents but are forced to attend schools in faraway districts. No, Alex, I really do not think this was the *raison d'etre* for busing. I think it might be a good idea to leave this topic to me; not that I'm a great expert, but I was, after all, educated in America. If pressed on the subject during interviews, simply observe that you are not *for* busing so much as *against* segregation, and if the court determines that busing can be an antidote to legal segregation, then you will go along with that.

P.P.S. I am told that your polemic is appreciably improved, but you still wear your polyester Russian outfits. Must I explain every detail? Your rayon clothes will be deeply embarrassing to the upscale crowd in which you are now moving. They expect you to be ahead of your time. Get yourself some button-downs and Guccis.

My dear Alex:

Did you know that "One obvious meaning of the Cross is unilateral disarmament"? I didn't. But I have come across just this opinion from Archbishop Raymond Hunthausen of Seattle. Alex, I am sure your suspicions about the American Catholic Church will abate somewhat when you learn more about this fellow. Reading his works, I get the definite impression that he regards the nuclear arms race as more ominous than atheism. In a very progressive gesture, the Archbishop has decided not to pay 50 percent of his federal taxes as a protest against what he calls "nuclear murder and suicide."

You know my reservations about the unilateral disarmament advocates. And yet Archbishop Hunthausen is symbolic of a powerful movement within the churches to help our country achieve its objectives. Not only do many of the prominent spokesmen for the churches want arms control treaties signed, but they are also challenging age-old suspicions about our country and our leaders. Here is former Congressman Father Robert Drinan: "The only hope for the lessening of the possibility of a nuclear war is for the lessening of the tensions and hostility that brought it about in the first place—the fear of Communism by the American people."

Drinan also uses the very effective device of rationalizing our invasion of Afghanistan by minimizing our gains there. "Even in Afghanistan, resistance is vigorous to the attempt to Sovietize that backward country. The people of Afghanistan, furthermore, are fearlessly independent; they have been fighting off outsiders since Alexander the Great, Genghis Khan, and the Mongol and British Empires." Drinan goes on to note that "The trend of Soviet influence has not been increasing; it has been static or even declining."

Obviously *we* cannot make these arguments, but I am kicking myself that they had not occurred to me. It is exactly the kind of thing we want: rhetoric that subtly changes the subject, that refuses to acknowledge our victories so that we may have more of them, rhetoric that focuses on *American* evils and *American* pathologies—including the "inordinate fear of Communism," as Jimmy Carter put it.

You are probably suspicious of this sort of reasoning. With your rigorous training in logic, you wonder whether people will really buy this absurd calculus, by which our complete and undeniable conquests are counted as staggering defeats by the American left. I agree, sometimes the left is too blatant. Arthur Macy Cox in his book *Russian Roulette* calls our invasion of Afghanistan and our support for the Vietnamese invasion of Cambodia "a disastrous setback for the highest priorities of Soviet national security policy." I wish Cox and the dilettante left would leave these subtle arguments to the big boys, Drinan and Noam Chomsky and (ever dependable) Tony Lewis.

I hope that by now you have read the Catholic bishops' pastoral letter on nuclear war. There is some careful qualifying language in it, but for heaven's sake, don't attack these sections; we are far better off if we ignore them, and create the impression that this is a moral clarion call for disarmament, an ecclesiastical repudiation of Michael Novak and Bill Buckley. After all, the pastoral letter is now in our hands and the hands of the American media to amplify. Let's do to it what we did to Vatican II: interpret it as entirely congenial to our position, so that orthodox Catholics will feel that they have to choose between their church and disarmament, on the one hand, and right-wing anti-Communism, on the other.

Sincerely yours,

Vladimir

P.S. The strategic defense debate is heating up. Could you return to me that Mary McGrory column on "Star Wars" that I sent you? I have been straining to come up with arguments for why it is not in the U.S.'s interest to defend itself against a Soviet missile attack. But no arguments occur to me, and I have to fall back on McGrory's ingenuity on this one.

My dear Alex:

I find little Samantha Smith as repulsive as you do. Still, it would be wise to avoid describing her as possessing "a peanut-shaped forehead, littered by a clump of what appears to be greasy rat hair."

Remember, this 11-year-old schoolgirl wrote personally to our great leader, Yuri Andropov, expressing her deep fears about the nuclear arms race. Her tour of our country will illustrate graphically our commitment to peace. On her return, she can appear on the Phil Donahue and Johnny Carson shows minimizing any differences between our systems and stressing that "everyone was *so* nice" during her visit. I was against the whole thing initially, figuring that it was too transparent. But I forgot that over here, children are special—treated with reverence, and immune to the kind of rigorous, realistic training provided by a good socialist education.

One sour note: There is an unfortunately skeptical piece on Samantha's visit in this week's issue of *U.S. News and World Report*, written by Nicholas Daniloff. The headline to the piece is, "Samantha Smith—Pawn in Propaganda War," and it gets worse after that. "Why Samantha and not any of the other Americans who have written letters to Andropov?" Daniloff writes. "The answer: Letters are carefully screened, and her opposition to nuclear war fitted into the Kremlin's war of words with the administration . . . No matter what her well-meant intentions, Samantha's message to Andropov is being used here to tell the Soviet people that average Americans want peace but are being pushed in the opposite direction by their government."

Unfortunately, we have to deal with these agitators more carefully than in the old days, Alex, when someone like Daniloff would have been chucked swiftly. So I'd like you to start a file of his articles—similar to the one we kept on Andrew Nagorski of *Newsweek* last year before we ejected him. Sooner or later, one of those KGB clowns at the United Nations or the Washington Embassy will slip up and get caught, and when he does, voila! Nicholas Daniloff will be a "propaganda pawn" himself.

Sincerely yours,

Vladimir

My dear Alex:

So you really think our shooting down of the airliner was a "brilliant demonstration of Soviet skills," do you? Despite your improvement, I sometimes despair of you, Alex.

There truly was no excuse for the downing of KAL 007. Our own response has been hopelessly delayed due to the weak condition of several of the Politburo members. We are left to fish for our own explanations.

Please don't deny any Soviet involvement in this matter. Stay away from the position of *The Nation* that "While there is no doubt that the Soviet Union's act of downing an unarmed civilian airliner was the proximate cause of the loss of 269 lives, the U.S. government must be held accountable and accept its share of the blame." We can't always follow these guys, Alex. And you have to remember that they are so consistently pro-Soviet that they don't have very much credibility in America. Pass on this one.

From the evidence it seems that we did open fire on an unarmed plane and kill the civilians on board. Certainly you can point out that the evidence so far is inconclusive. But the most important thing is to make sure that this incident remains only a minor, temporary embarrassment, and not a major obstacle.

Therefore, in response to your specific questions:

1. Yes, I think it is all right to praise President Reagan's lack of retaliation. Yet you might note that he seems anxious to "jump to the conclusion" that the Soviets shot down a plane. That way, whatever facts emerge are almost irrelevant—the point will be that Reagan is eager to "blame the Soviet Union first."

2. Your reaction to the stand taken by such politicians as Walter Mondale and Gary Hart surprises me. So they have criticized Reagan for reacting weakly to the incident. But this is because these men are anxious to establish that they are tough in the same way that Reagan is keen to prove that he is peaceful.

I think you are making a grave error when you suggest that Mondale and Hart's criticisms prove that they have defected from our side to Reagan's side. It is a mistake to think that because these people often support policies that coincide with ours, their intentions are the same as ours. You seem to think that we have achieved some kind of elaborate, indirect conspiracy. This is not how it works at all.

Indeed, that is the wonder of it. We do not have to issue instructions to our friends on the left, we simply take our cues from them. Thus, in nine cases out of ten, we can show up at the same restaurant, at the same time, sit at the same table, and order the same dinner, and still be able to honestly say, "Fancy meeting you here."

3. Do not be too worried about what to say if you are asked to appear on TV, as you surely will be. The main thing is to say it calmly, peacefully. Do that, and the facts will be forgotten in a few weeks. Hungary, Czechoslovakia, Berlin, Afghanistan—KAL 007 too, shall pass.

By the way, Alex, I want to send Jane Pauley a congratulations card for the birth of her baby, but have lost her address. Do you have it?

Sincerely yours,

Vladimir

P.S. Good news. It looks like the Democrats are going to make significant gains in the election next year. Have a bottle of wine on me, but don't forget that our main target is the man coming up for the top spot in 1984.

My dear Alex:

Well, it looks as if Reagan doesn't plan anything serious over the jetliner. Whew! I thought the old goat would at least kick a few of our KGB agents out of the United Nations. Instead, nothing. Looks as if Andre and Stanislov won't have to sublet their place on West 71st Street after all. Did you see some of their frantic cables back to Moscow?

In any event, the Kremlin has asked me for an explanation of what happened; naturally, my explanation gives a great deal of credit to you and me, Alex. It was our tireless work over the last few years, particulary mine, that helped create an atmosphere in which Reagan was convinced there was nothing he could do.

You might want to add the following entries to the old sanctions-don't-work file. *The New Republic:* "Sanctions against the Soviets never work." (Remember, Alex, this magazine has been getting more and more anti-Soviet of late; their pragmatic advice on how to fight us has great credibility.) *National Review:* "The sort of sanctions many have been suggesting would have shifted the focus from the crime itself to a quarrel over the wisdom and the efficacy of the sanctions." Conservative TV host John McLaughlin: "Such tactics would be temporary at best, requiring early or late reversal . . . They would entail hopeless policy, hurt us more than the Soviets, breed division among our allies and squabbles in Congress, and, most important, defeat the larger purpose of building international public opprobium towards the Soviets." (You can say all that about nearly any action the United States might take against us, and I plan to do so.)

I don't know about you, Alex, but my favorite remedy for these periods of "international public opprobium" is to eat a good steak and spend a week or two at the beach—especially after a hot summer like this one. Does that answer your question about whether to cancel your speech next week, comparing U.S. and Soviet legal systems, at Dartmouth College? Don't be silly. I was at Dartmouth last year and got a glowing introduction from the school's president, David McLaughlin. Dave is one of those bourgeois bureaucrats, a man who means well feebly. He's much too well-mannered to make any remarks about our air defense shooting down a couple of hundred civilians.

So go to Hanover, have a nice time, and above all, say hello for me to Marysa Navarro—the woman professor who has spoken so glowingly of life in Cuba. She's not one of those faint-hearted types who gave up on Castro in the 1970s, mind you, but a real, committed Fidel-backer. While you're up there, you might also see if you can pick up a couple copies of an underground newspaper called *The Dartmouth Review*, a weekly put out by some of the reactionary, pro-Reagan students there. According to my sources, it's really fun to read, and I notice that these anti-Soviet samizdats are popping up at a lot of other campuses. It's probably something we need to look into.

Sincerely yours,

Vladimir

My dear Alex:

Let me put your mind to rest about Afghanistan. You want to know whether it is really true, as industrialist Armand Hammer informed *The New York Times* not long ago, that "the Soviet ambassador to the United States, Anatoly F. Dobrynin, told him the Soviet Union planned to withdraw its troops from Afghanistan." You note that Dan Rather has reported, "there are indications . . . that the Soviet Army may be looking for a way to disentangle itself from Afghanistan." You worry about an assessment by Senator Gary Hart that Afghanistan could prove "a Soviet Vietnam," and about Selig Harrison's assessment in *USA Today* that "as the diplomatic, military, and economic costs of its involvement have grown, Moscow has searched for . . . a way out."

Really, Alex, there is nothing to worry about. Our troops control all the major cities and roads. A tough but small resistance movement is holding out in the hills, and getting some aid from the United States. So far, however, the amounts are small, and much of the aid has been mishandled anyway. Still, it would be nice to cut of the assistance completely, and crush the resistance. So we have been putting out the line that our withdrawal may be imminent. Perhaps a token withdrawal of a few thousand troops is all that is needed to convince the West of our sincerity.

In fact, many people in the West understand that our invasion of Afghanistan was a legitimate act of self-defense. Craig Whitney of *The New York Times* says: "Seen from the inside, the Soviet motivation seems more like military defensiveness, caused by historic Russian fear of encirclement by hostile forces . . . A senior Western diplomat here noted that in a recent meeting, Foreign Minister Andrei A. Gromyko seemed almost obsessed by a threat to Soviet security from the United States and China."

Tom Wicker of *The New York Times* blames our fear of Mohammed: "With the Islamic world in a sort of religious revival, the last thing the Soviets wanted was a fundamentalist Moslem government in Kabul. That might well have meant trouble among the 50 million Soviet Moslems . . . So the Soviets brought in their tanks and helicopters."

Alex, you should understand the value of our leaders' fear. There is always something for us to be afraid of. Now that our troops are in Afghanistan, we must worry about the supply of arms reaching our enemies through Pakistan, right? And shouldn't we also worry about protecting our sea routes to Pakistan's traditional rival, our friend and ally, India? Won't we need to be even more concerned about China? And what about Iran itself—isn't it a fundamentalist Moslem state, at war with our ally Iraq, and a potential ally of the Moslem fanatics in Afghanistan?

I could go on and on, but I think you get the point. Alex, we could make it all the way to North Dakota—and there would still be the hostile borders in Minnesota, Montana, and South Dakota for our generals to be afraid of. This fear of encirclement drove the Romans all the way to Britain in search of security. If Rome had been smart enough to hire somebody like me, they'd have started to worry then about Norway, Iceland, Canada . . .

Sincerely yours,

Vladimir

My dear Alex:

Thank you for sending me the copy of Richard Nixon's latest book, *Real Peace*. I must admit at first, it struck me as nothing new. After all, Nixon has always called for things like "detente with deterrence" and a "tough, realistic foreign policy." The Americans were bombing Hanoi and Cambodia right through some of the Paris talks; indeed, Nixon and Kissinger admit in their memoirs that some of the bombings were specifically timed to coincide with their public peace offensives. So it all seemed to me to be, well, more of the same old stuff.

Your underlinings, and your attached memo, however, have shown me the light. I can see how, quoted correctly, one can contrast Nixon's buzzwords with Reagan's foreign policy *actions*. Because Nixon spends so much time puffing up Reagan, I had not even seen that possibility.

Indeed, you seem to have gotten well ahead of the whole crowd on this one. It wasn't until several days after your letter that I saw all the op-ed pieces fawning on Nixon as a "statesman." Are you sure Nixon has been invited to speak before the National Press Club? This is such a pretty development I hardly know what to say. The same people who destroyed his Presidency are now building him up as the great pragmatist, simply because he would operate a foreign policy a little bit to the left of Reagan's. How resourceful. The whole concept has me so excited, I'm ordering a copy of Barry Goldwater's latest speeches to see if I can find any similar material.

Keep up the perceptive work. You have grown.

Sincerely yours,

Vladimir

My dear Alex:

Your latest letter on our loss in Grenada reveals that you are a slow learner.

Your refer to Grenada as an "unimportant country" and a "tiny piece of real estate." You say that you cannot understand why this situation is being treated as a tragedy among our superiors in Moscow.

Alex, haven't you ever heard of the Brezhnev Doctrine? For years, America has tacitly accepted Brezhnev's claim that "What's ours is ours and what is theirs is negotiable." Before Grenada, not an inch of our soil had fallen into the Western camp. Moreover, the incomparable Fidel had Grenada solidly on our side and had taught them all the tricks you learned back in the Lenin School: cracking down on domestic opposition, assisting fellow revolutionary brothers fighting Reagan's democracies in Latin America and the Caribbean, and so on.

Even our allies in Congress realize the gravity of the situation in Grenada. For instance, did you hear the comments of Democrat Ted Weiss of New York on the floor of the House after Grenada? He said, "The President's invasion of Grenada is . . . an impeachable offense." What a guy!

Former American Ambassador to the U.N. Andrew Young said that "what we have is an aging and failing President. We shouldn't risk American lives for saving face."

And Jesse Jackson (he's the black fellow I told you about—a great admirer of Fidel) said that Americans "ought to be outraged . . . (I call for) an immediate cessation of military action against Grenada and reparations to the Grenadian people for damages caused by this invasion."

No doubt some of this will sound a bit extreme to you, Alex, but at least it should help you realize that a lot is at stake here.

Sincerely yours,

Vladimir

P.S.   I was pleased to hear of your invitation to the Common Cause reception at the New York Waldorf. If you see my old friend Fred Wertheimer, don't forget to tell him that I sent fifteen bucks in response to his last direct mail appeal. Out of my own money! I better get my Jerry Falwell dartboard in the mail next week.

My dear Alex:

Well, this is not our year is it? First the American economy recovers, and now this Grenada business. I'm afraid my long Christmas vacation may be down the tubes.

While I understand your frustration with Gary Hart, Walter Mondale, and John Glenn, I'm compelled to tell you we cannot expect much from them. In fact, I'm rather surprised they have gone as far as they have in criticizing the invasion; even Tip O'Neill has more or less supported what Reagan is doing.

A long time ago, I warned you about this: The Americans may squabble with one another, but the minute a President calls them to action, all sorts of things that could be said are no longer respectable, and the country unites. It is rather fortunate that for so long after Vietnam, American leaders themselves actually forgot this. In this respect, the party line in Moscow is correct. The Americans really are very willing to make war, provided their pathetic ideology tells them it is for a worthy cause.

Rather than urging Gary, Walter, and John to sacrifice themselves on this issue, then, we should be as quiet as possible. Let them make their show of patriotic support for Reagan and save their fodder for more important battles.

Besides, we always have the Europeans. If you're determined to write something on this, why don't you concentrate on their reaction? Do the old even-the-U.S.-allies-oppose-this-policy job. I have some good quotes on file from Margaret Thatcher, who is anxious to distance herself from Reagan in order to broaden her domestic appeal. Don't say that, of course, but do commend her for "trying to steer the U.S. towards peace and away from confrontation."

I rather liked your suggestion that we interpret the invasion as a move by the United States to shore up "what it seems to regard as a sphere of influence." You see, Americans are historically very bad at balance-of-power politics. They need a mission—say, establishing their own democratic system in other countries—in order to support any kind of intervention. One of the turning points in Vietnam, in fact, was when Johnson and then Nixon framed the war not in terms of spreading freedom but in terms of "preventing a major defeat" to American commitments. This was a formulation that could easily be attacked on moral grounds. By contrast, fighting for democracy, though it seems silly to you and me, is one argument I have never been able to argue against except in the most sophisticated circles.

The best theme for us on Grenada, I feel, is that the U.S. is acting as a kind of bully. The beauty of this, given that the U.S. is sure to win easily, is that the better the American military is able to perform, the more the puny insignificance of a country like Grenada is brought to light.

But whatever happens, do not let yourself get too frustrated. Console yourself with looking at the broader picture, catch up on your reading, and relax. I hear National Public Radio is considering a six-part series on American uses of force in the 20th century. Maybe they can work in Grenada, with a note that it illustrates the "impulse to shoot now, negotiate later" that "seems to dominate the Reagan White House."

Sincerely yours,

Vladimir

My dear Alex:

It is hard to fully get over my post-Grenada blues, and yet I take solace in Senator Pat Moynihan's latest comments, which indicate a profound transformation in his thinking.

Moynihan, you will remember, was one of the most prominent members of the so-called Jackson wing of the Democratic Party, and a real pain in the neck to us. I vividly remember that speech to the United Nations in which Moynihan said our diplomats live "in a world of lies." And the man called President Nixon's detente "a form of disguised retreat." I am enclosing a copy of Moynihan's 1975 article in *Commentary* blaming liberals for "actively participating in the sustained assault on American institutions." (This article should be sent to our superiors in Moscow, along with some of Moynihan's more recent writings, as evidence of our effectiveness in this country.)

I must say, even though I have followed Moynihan's gradual defection from the anti-Communist arm of the Democratic Party, I did not expect him to call Reagan's invasion of Grenada "bringing in democracy at the point of a bayonet." I was also pleasantly surprised to see his liberal rating by the Americans for Democratic Action (ADA) go up to 100 percent last year.

We don't need to know why Moynihan has ceased to threaten our foreign policy. Perhaps he wants to neutralize his left-wing opposition in the Democratic Party in New York. Perhaps he wants adulation in the East Coast media. What is significant is that Moynihan has changed. Did you see his recent piece in *Newsday* titled "Reagan MX Plan Commits U.S. to First Strike Policy"? Moynihan noted that "The result of MX deployment will be a world set on a hair trigger, ready to be catapulted into holocaust one day on about nine minutes' notice." Incredible. I must wait a few more months to make sure Pat is not just on an extended hangover, and then inform the KGB to revise our briefing papers, which somewhat antiquatedly refer to Moynihan as "an enemy of world socialism."

I bring up Moynihan's case, Alex, because what we are witnessing is nothing less than the collapse of the anti-Communist wing of the Democratic Party. Senator Henry Jackson—that infernal pest—is gone, and Moynihan has converted. Almost all the influential Congressmen in the Democratic Party are now advocates of appeasement. And the rising stars of the party—Steve Solarz of New York, Chris Dodd of Connecticut, Thomas Downey of Long Island, Edward Markey of Massachusetts—are even more sympathetic to us than their predecessors. Alex, we have nearly succeeded in shattering the anti-Communist consensus that has characterized U.S. foreign policy since World War II. This is historic. I am really getting excited. We can afford to lose Grenada if we are going to gain the whole of the Democratic Party.

Sincerely yours,

Vladimir

December 1983

My dear Alex:

We are getting close to 1984, and that, of course, means we are getting close to *1984:* a series of articles in the popular and academic press noting that "this is the year" that Orwell was talking about, and raising the usual questions and comparisons about his work and the condition of American society. People like you and me are certain to be drawn into this discussion, so knowing your tendency toward blunders, I am writing you in advance of this cascade to keep you from getting all wet.

First, you should be aware that a good deal of revisionist literary criticism has been going on in the West which has removed many of the toxic implications of Orwell that you were trained to resist. Several respected authors, for example (see attached clips), have helpfully written that it is actually the unchecked spread of technology and corporate power that Orwell was warning against, not the rise of the totalitarian state. Others have interpreted *1984* as a *cri de coeur* against, not totalitarianism, but right-wing fascism. Thank goodness we were able to establish Hitler a long time ago as an aberration of the right, rather than the "national socialist" he called himself.

Still, you are likely to run into someone who will press the Orwell point home, someone well read in the literature of the gulag and able to cite names of dissident leaders off the top of his head. In that case, the first thing to do is to sneer at the general notion that Orwell was talking about the Soviet Union at all. You will have a lot of mainstream scholarship working for you, and words like "paranoia" will be in your favor. You might say that, "whatever Orwell had in mind, my travels in America today suggest that if there is a threat of 1984 coming to pass, it is from the American right, with their

49

book burnings and threat of censorship and state religion."

My own view is that Orwell, closely read, is not that damaging to us. This is unorthodox, but let me explain. Orwell's horror show is, frankly, a bit too horrifying to be really horrible. It is an exaggeration of even the worst police state that has ever existed. Since *1984* is clearly worse than anything that has happened, anything real tends to pale by comparison. Thank goodness, in a way, that Orwell wrote such a chilling standard for others to live up to. After all, who needs the sweaty labor camps when the quiet mental hospitals are so much more effective?

If a Western writer ever really wants to damage socialism, in my opinion, he will not whip up any police beatings or bedroom cameras at all. A really effective attack on Communism would paint us not blood red, but gray. No guns, no starvations, no forced marches—just long lines and dull magazines, and very coarse toilet paper. I know you will continue to be discreet with these very personal comments.

Sincerely yours,

Vladimir

My dear Alex:

Time magazine has recently devoted a cover story to the "sins of the press." It notes a decline of confidence in the press, clearly evidenced by enormous public support for excluding the media from Reagan's invasion of Grenada. Boy, that was a wily move on the administration's part. Just think, Alex, if Dan Rather and Tom Brokaw were allowed to cover that operation! We would see lurid pictures of bodies; we would have interviews with the random retards accidentally bombed by the U.S. planes. The American public would be queasy, and support for the President would be quickly eroded.

Well, I don't want to be too lugubrious about Grenada. I just hope the media is able to pressure the Reagan administration to reverse its news coverage policy. The best hope lies in the so-called pragmatists in the White House, Jim Baker and Michael Deaver, who attach great importance to what is said on the editorial page of *The Washington Post*. They can probably be talked into a new set of rules for media coverage of future operations, in return for a few flattering profiles noting their profound concern for constitutional principles.

I know you are ambivalent about the media. Fortunately, you have matured since your arrival in this country. I remember an early letter in which you observed that "It strikes me as impossible that propaganda can coexist with a free press, and therefore our first goal must be to eliminate the American media." No doubt even you will smile when you remember this.

There is some merit in your concern that through press freedom is the highest doctrine of our journalistic colleagues here, it is incompatible with the progressive state we—and they—wish to establish. But, Alex, that is an enthusiasm that we can deal with later, by persuasion if possible, by coercion if necessary. Why worry about the spoils before we have won the war?

Remember, we are not theoreticians but propagandists. We are not primarily interested in the psychology of American reporters. Whatever their intentions, the fact is that they frequently bring their recommendations into practical alliance with our interests. The best example I can think of is the Falklands War. Remember all those articles in the press about how the U.S. was supporting a fascist dictatorship that tramples human rights? Well, all that yelling immediately subsided when the U.S. took the side of Britain during the Falklands War, and we sided with Argentina.

The crucial point about the American media is that it always discovers circuitous routes to back up our country's interests. It is precisely because they are headed in the same direction as we are, and because they are not viewed as part of the team, that they are so valuable. Personally we may despise them and call them dupes, but professionally we must respect them.

You can see I am buoyant about the American press. That is why I am a little disgruntled that you have not courted them some more. They are sore after this Grenada ban, so this is an excellent time to write columns about the "disturbing trend away from the adversary journalism of the 1960s and 1970s." Perhaps you can observe that it is "open season" on reporters under President Reagan. A phrase which never fails is "shooting the messenger for bringing the bad news."

A word about Ted Koppel: You are scheduled to make your second "Nightline" appearance soon. The debate with Buckley was, at best, a draw. Bill is always effective, but I think it was Koppel's probing questions that had you most bewildered. Koppel is, unfortunately, a fairly objective journalist, and a scathing interviewer. I have had my own difficult moments with him.

Don't be discouraged, however, because the most important point is that we get free publicity. Anytime we can show our face, it tends to undercut the American fear of Soviet intentions, and establish subliminally (the best way) that we are Real People, regular guys you could have a beer with, and not monsters in trenchcoats. It does not matter so much that we are forced to field inconvenient questions about slave labor camps. We are afforded the respectability of appearing on nationwide TV next to other reasonably civilized people. This image will counteract a thousand facts and figures, however devastating, that anyone debating us could possibly present.

Sincerely yours,

Vladimir

My dear Alex:

Didn't I once tell you that, on the right occasion, conservatives can be our best friends? If you didn't believe me, pick up the latest *U.S. News and World Report* in which Ronald Reagan wishes he hadn't said that the Soviet Union is an "evil empire," and says that reaching an arms control treaty is the top priority today for his administration.

It's vital for us, in the coming days, to praise Reagan for this comment, for it amounts to a major reversal. It is better, in a way, than if Reagan had simply never adopted a hard line in the first place. Now, he has said it and backed off. His supporters will be sneered at when they adopt a similar line. Indeed, I have the feeling that the term "evil empire" will now be a positive weapon in our hands.

For example: Pat Buchanan asks you about arms shipments to Nicaragua. You say that is Castro's business, we do not interfere. Buchanan says, "How do you expect us to believe there's no connection between you and Castro's arms to the Sandinistas?" You say, "Oh, come on Pat; are you trying to resurrect the 'evil empire' theory, which even Ronald Reagan has abandoned?" You see?

This doesn't mean we cannot express skepticism, even while praising "the pragmatic side of Reagan." In fact, it's important that we demand "actions, not just words" to see if the U.S. is "really sincere about its intentions to finally return to the process of detente."

I wish I could be as encouraged about the Democrats. None of them has much of a chance, I fear, as long as the American economy is in good shape and the country is at peace. Did you see Ted Koppel interviewing them the other night up at Dartmouth? What a disgrace. Hart and Mondale got bogged down in a debate over which one of them was the first to support the nuclear freeze. Both railed on about a balanced budget and the Reagan deficits. I never have understood enough about the Americans' crazy economic system to know whether "the deficits" are really good, as the Democrats usually claim, or bad, as Reagan used to claim. But I do notice two things: 1. They seem to have little to do with the economy and, in fact, often seem to help (maybe we should run some deficits in Moscow); and, 2. Whatever political party is making a big stink about them seems to do very badly in the elections.

The more I consider it, though, the more there is hope that Reagan may not be so bad for us after all. A quiet breathing spell, during which we suffer a few minor setbacks, but our military keeps getting stronger, our recent gains (such as Nicaragua) are solidified, and so on. Only Star Wars really frightens me, and when the time is right, we will get Reagan to trade it away.

You, of course, cannot remember, but there was a time when both Nixon and Eisenhower sounded just as tough as Reagan on foreign policy; in fact, Eisenhower actually sent the Marines into Lebanon, and Nixon sent his forces, however ineffectively, into Cambodia and Laos. But we survived— because those of us who were here concentrated on limiting the damage.

So don't be glum. And do follow up on that Louis Farrakhan fellow. I love his comments about the Jews. Is he really black, and a very hardline preacher? Maybe there is some way we can link him to the Republicans; wouldn't that be fun? Although I'm losing heart about the chances of defeating Reagan, it is always important to keep the old boy on the defensive.

Sincerely yours,

Vladimir

My dear Alex:

Just received your note in the mail enclosing Tony Lewis' latest column. You're confused that he seems to be lamenting the decline of the NATO alliance. You thought he was on our side, you say, and want to know whether I was misleading your all the time. I read Lewis' column and, I must say, was initially baffled by it. But then I realized that something must be wrong, so I re-read the piece, and my respect for Tony was confirmed once again. He is simply miles ahead of us, Alex. You see, this column was worrying about the divisions within NATO in order to advocate that strong-willed members such as the U.S. should bring their foreign policy into line with their most weak-willed, appeasement-minded NATO members. Simply brilliant!

I see you are despondent now that the Western alliance has begun to put in the Pershings. Still, your lamentations about our "great and probably irreversible defeat" are wildly overstated. I admit that our loss on this issue constitutes a psychological setback, but only because we came so close to total victory. As for your extreme recommendation that we spend more money encouraging violent demonstrations, I cannot imagine a more self-defeating policy. I am convinced that it was this sort of heavy-handed interventionism by the Central Committee that guaranteed our defeat on this issue. I know that the chairman was determined to use a more subtle approach, but there are still those in the Kremlin who refuse to let Andropov be Andropov.

A few thoughts:

1. Really, there has been no "Western victory." Five years ago we had a substantial advantage in nuclear weapons in Europe. Today, that advantage is larger. Five years

from now it will be still larger. Warmonger Reagan himself has admitted that when all the Pershing and Cruise
deployments are completed, they will not equal the
number of warheads the U.S. unilaterally destroyed in
the 1970s. What has happened is that the West has
decided, at least for now, to keep its weakness within
tolerable bounds. They have resolved to maintain a Eu-
ropean deterrent. In other words, we failed to achieve
what could have been a substantial gain, but we lost
nothing. The U.S. and its allies, under the most reactionary set of leaders in recent history, narrowly escaped
checkmate. But we still have the better pieces on the
board.

2. Given this, the fact that the West is so exultant is a good
thing. From your training, you are used to using despair
as a psychological tool, and it has important uses. Yet
euphoria can be just as useful, indeed better, because
a happy drunk will want to remain drunk, and get drunk
again, while an angry drunk quickly focuses on the cause
of his unhappiness. So the Americans are happy about
not surrendering, and Reagan is bragging about the
country "standing tall"? Fine. I will begin to worry about
all this when there are nuclear freeze rallies in Moscow,
or contras in Eastern Europe. Meanwhile, our battles
with the West continue to end in one of two ways: a win
for us, or a draw.

3. I must say, I have been planning for some time on the
assumption that the Cruise and Pershing missiles would
be emplaced. I knew they would go in the day we decided to send money to the freeze movement. That is
why I am already congratulating my friends in the churches
and the media on the "American victory." In the first
place, it embarrasses them; they are forced to come back
and say, "Well I just hope that your leaders will still be

willing to negotiate, Vlady; none of us benefits from this madness."

Second, it encourages them to think that they have won a victory. Soon they will begin to wonder: what have we won, except another expensive step in the arms race? Then it will be time to remind them that the whole reason for building the missiles was to give President Reagan what he called a "needed bargaining chip" in arms negotiations. Count on someone to write a column noting that "Six months after the placement of missiles in Europe, America is no closer than before to an arms control agreement, which was the justification for building those missiles in the first place."

Then it will be time for us to remind everyone not only that there has been no arms control progress, but unfortunately the placement of missiles in Europe has strengthened the hands of our own hawks in the Kremlin—make sure to concede that "we have our militarists too"—and made it much harder for us pragmatists to get our comrades to do business with President Reagan. Soon somebody will float the idea that a temporary halt to the deployment of the Euromissiles should be enacted "to see if the Soviets perhaps are interested in making a reciprocal gesture." Arms talks will reconvene, and within a few months George Bush will be giving speeches defending the moratorium on the very missiles that were such a "victory" not long ago.

You see how it works, Alex? In Western politics what is done is often less important than why it is done. If the missiles stay in, but we can erode the idea that they are there to prevent an attack by our forces, then we have accomplished a far more important task. We have eroded the will of the West at the very same time that the West has convinced itself that it is being tough. Soon after that, the missiles themselves will go. They are only a material reflection of the West's willingness to defend itself.

So don't worry about the current bouyant mood in Washington. It is only a sober calculation of forces, and a patient application of them, that we need fear. Euphoria and fear, euphoria and despair—this cycle is hardly our enemy; it is precisely what we want to encourage.

Sincerely yours,

Vladimir

P.S.   In your debate on arms control, I notice the figures you use to describe the nuclear balance are those presented in TASS. I know those are the numbers we are told to use, but frankly, Americans will not be convinced by them. *The New York Times* did a chart which you should memorize and use instead. Their numbers have much more credibility, and besides, the *Times* chart shows a much greater U.S. advantage in most areas. And don't forget after citing a few comparisons to say something like "as if these numbers meant anything anyway."

P.P.S.   Remember I was telling you about the old anti-communist tradition in the Democratic Party? Listen to this. "The enemy is the communist system itself—implacable, insatiable, unceasing in its drive for world domination. This is not a struggle for the supremacy of arms alone. It is also a struggle for supremacy between two conflicting ideologies: freedom under God versus ruthless, godless tyranny." (John F. Kennedy, 1960 campaign speech). "I believe it must be the policy of the United States to support free peoples who are resisting attempted subjugation by armed minorities or by outside pressures." (Harry Truman, speech to joint session of Congress, 1947).

I pass these along, Alex, because you should be prepared in case any of the neoconservatives chuck them in your face.

After all, contrast the above with what the new liberals are saying. "We are not free of that inordinate fear of communism . . . I believe in detente with the Soviet Union. We hope that the Soviet Union will join in playing a larger role in aiding the developing world, for common aid efforts will help us build a bridge of mutual confidence." (Jimmy Carter, speech at Notre Dame, 1977). "It may take the destruction of Western civilization to allow the rest of the world to emerge as a free and brotherly society." (Andrew Young, quoted in *Congressional Record*, 1977). "Castro does not seem to be a dictator for his own sake, but a convinced revolutionary who is popular among his people." (George McGovern in his book *Grassroots*). "I don't think we ought to automatically assume that a self-determined Marxist government is something we can't stand." (Gary Hart, quoted in *The Washington Post*, February 1984).

My dear Alex:

You see? No sooner did your whimpering about the Cruise missile deployments subside than the Congress here voted to make production of the MX missile contingent upon our refusal to negotiate at arms talks. All we have to do is walk up to the table and smile: there goes the MX.

I must say I was not very much amused by the way you hooted with laughter over my suggestion over the phone that you explain our use of biological warfare in Afghanistan— yellow rain—by saying that the natives are simply victims of "bee droppings." I assure you, Alex, that this is a serious argument in the U.S. and a Harvard biochemist Matthew Meselson, has endorsed it. (No, I don't know whether he is one of ours, but make sure to use the term "leading" whenever you quote him, which should be frequently.)

Your own explanation of yellow rain—that the chemicals were dropped by the CIA to embarrass the Soviet Union— isn't bad, but why try and work up enthusiasm for this somewhat predictable line of argument, when we have Meselson's exotic hypothesis to work with? Apparently, the American intelligentsia, which desperately wants to believe that we are living up to arms control agreements so that they can sign more of them, is willing to stretch credibility and embrace the bee droppings line. So let's go with the flow, comrade.

The Pope assassination stuff worries me, Alex. I know the Americans are stupid. They want to think it was anyone but we who were behind this one. How I wish that were true. We really should refrain from this crude, anachronistic behavior. I know the Pope was causing us trouble with his inspiration of Solidarity in Poland—those damn unions: get rid of them, I always said—but if this assassination attempt is traced through Bulgaria, it's going to be much worse than our shooting down the airliner. Imagine if President Reagan got the information to the Catholics in Latin America! Oh dear. We should give utmost priority to encouraging the Americans who are trying to discredit the reporter Claire Sterling who broke the story, such as Michael Dobbs of *The Washington Post*, and Alex Cockburn of *The Nation*. Can any of our respectable foundations give Dobbs and Cockburn an award for fellowship, recognize their contribution to humanity and that sort of thing? I really don't think we have the votes on the Pulitzer committee this year.

To add to my headaches, Reagan has just announced his candidacy for reelection. Just as I feared he would. I don't think the Democrats can win this one on economic issues. Can you imagine why Mondale and Hart are concentrating on the federal deficit? I don't think anybody outside Washington cares about deficits, if indeed they know what they are. Republicans lost elections on this issue for half a century. Besides, who trusts Mondale more than Reagan to reduce government debt?

We have to attack Reagan on foreign policy, where he is vulnerable. Arms control and Central America should be the foci of the Democratic Party campaign. I am eagerly awaiting the airing of an ABC movie "The Day After," which apparently simulates a nuclear attack on a Kansas town. Why don't our people think up this kind of stuff, Alex?

Sincerely yours,

Vladimir

My dear Alex:

This will have to be short. As you must have suspected, I've been invited back to Moscow for the funeral. How depressing. First Brezhnev, now Andropov. And I hear Konstantin Chernenko is making a bid for succession; I might be back in Moscow again in a few months. How I wish you could go in my place. Did you know the Hotel Stalin has managed to find an even thinner brand of toilet paper than they had when you were interning at *Pravda?* The accommodations really are dreadful, quite an embarrassment when you have to entertain Dusko Doder of the *Post* and Craig Whitney of the *Times,* as I do.

Well, the good news for you is that I will be amending my last report on you to stress that you have made notable progress. You were particularly effective in dealing with the matter of that blasted Korean jetliner. Most important, you did not get bogged down in the facts, quickly moving on instead to "the far more important question of how our two countries can re-open a serious arms control dialog."

That is the way, my young friend: sting and float. Didn't you almost feel sorry for John Lofton, who took the bait? His pathetic citation of all the evidence from American newspapers that our superiors actually shot down an unarmed passenger plane must have bored even many American conservatives.

If there is anything I can do for you while I'm in Moscow, you can cable me at the hotel. And by the way: I'm passing your name along to Bob Semple at the *Times* op-ed page. He's always pestering me for young talent. I hope you will not let me down if he asks you to submit something.

Must run.

Sincerely yours,

Vladimir

My dear Alex:

A rather embarrassing situation has developed that could damage someone who has done a great deal for our cause: Carl Sagan. His recent articles on nuclear winter have created a tremendous stir. But his piece in *Foreign Affairs* contains a footnote which cites "independent corroboration" from leading Soviet scientists—even though there is no such corroboration of his work in print in the Soviet journals. I have been getting calls from Charles Mohr at *The New York Times* asking for copies of the studies, but it is hard to send him what doesn't exist.

For complicated reasons, I think Alexander Velikov, who did our work to verify the *Limits to Growth* study and is working to prove that strategic defense is impossible, told Sagan this spring that he would shortly be completing a paper on the matter. Sagan naturally took him at his word and began working him into the papers and articles now coming out. Typically, Velikov has been late getting that paper done. Idiot. All he has to do is rewrite Sagan's paper in Russian. But now Sagan is up a tree.

I'm sure I don't have to tell you how important the nuclear winter theory is to us. Basically, it states that any nuclear war, no matter who launches it, will cause the whole planet to freeze, and thus kill even the attacker. War is no longer "winnable." It's been a very useful theory, both here and in Europe. What is more, Sagan has become a leading critic of Star Wars on "scientific grounds." He and the Union of Concerned Scientists are publishing a paper sometime this spring showing that you cannot build a defense against nuclear weapons in space. We mustn't allow that kind of spokesman to be discredited.

What I'd like you to do is write a mild attack on Sagan, say a letter to the editor at *Foreign Affairs* or the *Times*, to the effect that he is only repeating conclusions about the devastating effects of nuclear war that Soviet scientists reached years ago. I'm enclosing a group of clips that talk in very scientific terms about soot and ashes and "the potential biological threat" from large-scale explosions. No one is likely to understand most of this stuff, Alex. But if anyone ever asks for more concrete statements about "winter" or "freezing," we will simply remind them that "unfortunately, our superiors in Moscow are very paranoid" and have refused to declassify this sensitive information.

When you've done this, see if you can round up Velikov—I think he's at a conference on the threat of first strike weapons over in Europe—and get him to finish the damn paper. Tell him not to worry about appearing original, but reach the same conclusions Sagan does with some slightly altered charts and graphs.

I really hate to dump this problem on you, but there's a conference on world banking going on and I've been invited to speak about opening up East-West trade opportunities. I thought I might comment on "the irony that it is Ronald Reagan, and not my own country, who seems determined to damage the efforts of U.S. bankers to aid the spread of free trade."

Sincerely yours,

Vladimir

My dear Alex:

URGENT: I strongly suggest you cancel your trip to Egypt, mentioned in your letter, at once.

REPEAT: Cancel trip to Egypt.

The embassy tells me that Cairo airport is due to take a major hit within the next few weeks. You will be in grave danger traveling through even for a day. It would be a terrible embarrassment for a Soviet journalist to get hit; we have maintained a record of virtually no casualties in terrorist attacks since expanding our initiatives in the 1970s.

I have told you before, Alex, to check with me, or with the embassy in Washington, to make sure your plans don't put you in any danger from our network. I only hope this letter reaches you in time.

—Vlady

My dear Alex:

You idiot. You absolute idiot. How could you publish an attack on President Reagan's proposed "Star Wars" strategic defense plan on the grounds that it "is a hopeless boondoggle and will only waste taxpayer money"? Don't you see that only our American sympathizers can make this argument, not you? Whose side are you on? If we lose on this vital issue, I really will have to worry about your future, comrade.

Nor did you help your career by being seen at the debate between Radosh-Milton and the Schneers on the guilt of the Rosenbergs. I turn on the TV and see you jumping up and down with glee at arguments in favor of the Rosenbergs launched by the Schneers. Really, Alex, I know you probably thought you were on your own time, but you are gravely embarrassing people like Victor Navasky who are valuable to us.

Perhaps an explanation for your blunders may be found in your recent request for my thoughts on whether you should address a group of Young Socialists at Harvard. Obviously, you are beginning to feel a bit demoralized, even though you have not been in this country very long. You fear that the Americans are truly a long way from the kind of revolutionary consciousness we have been able to foment elsewhere. It is only natural for you to want to recharge your batteries; this, perhaps, explains your enthusiasm for the Harvard group. There you won't be bothered with nasty questions about Stalin and Afghanistan and chemical weapons—in fact, several professors and students will certainly come out in favor of these things.

But the advantages of getting your anti-imperialist adrenalin flowing again are, in my opinion, far outweighed by the dangers posed by this appearance. Silly as it may seem, I think that the last thing the American socialists need is any support from us. I am getting increasingly worried, for example, about the money we have been pumping into the nuclear freeze movement, both here and in Europe. Such a strategy can only backfire when a clever U.S. politician such as Reagan finds out and begins to exploit our contributions to play on nationalistic fears. And since the amount of money we give is so small, and the movement could exist without it anyway, it seems clumsy to get involved in helping those who would do us more good out of the purest of motives by themselves.

We should not give the reactionaries any excuse to impugn the motives of our friends. Thus, any identification of yours with those students at Harvard would only hurt their cause. You must take the kind of attitude that Henry V took toward Falstaff, except that you must play Falstaff, and recognize that your own good friend cannot afford to be seen with you.

Why don't you spend a little less time thinking about a puny group of student socialists and see if you can't get that grant from the Mobil Oil Foundation to expand our engineering student exchange program? Oh, and regarding your other question, I would not waste three days at the AFL-CIO rally; they really are dreadful reactionaries. Labor, I am afraid, was really the wrong thing for Marx to focus upon. I will expound more on this theme later but right now there's a Bill Moyers special on the danger of mixing religion and politics posed by the fundamentalist New Right, and tomorrow I've been invited to address a group of Catholic bishops on the danger of poor communication between the superpowers. So I really must dash.

Sincerely yours,

Vladimir

My dear Alex:

The case of Andrei Sakharov is again surfacing in the West. What a nuisance. And yet I cannot help thinking that, because of the gusto with which *The New York Times* and *The Washington Post* praise Sakharov and condemn his oppressors, there has got to be something in it for us. Hmm.

Yes, I think I get it. For these papers to condemn our country for penalizing Sakharov is a way to appear evenhanded about attacking the U.S. and the Soviet Union. The main difference, of course, is that these papers have absolutely no effect on our leaders. In fact, it may be a good idea for us to increase the beatings of Sakharov and have that fact leak out, so that more indignant editorials may appear, and the Western press can establish its anti-Communist credentials. Then, on the issues that really matter—shooting down planes and negotiating arms treaties—they are with us and don't feel so bad about being with us.

For our leaders to hold on to some dissidents for too long can be a mistake, however. Take the case of Solzhenitsyn. Certainly we did the right thing about that pain in the neck. That man was single-handedly dismantling the great Soviet system that our leaders took 60 years to build. Now that we have let him go, look at the poor sop. He's a hermit in Vermont or something.

Don't you love the way the Western media handled Solzhenitsyn? They didn't nail him on the cross the way our comrades are attempting to do. Instead they laughed him out of existence. They told him he was "out of touch" with the "complex realities" of Western life. They said he who had lived in the gulag did not really understand "true freedom." While Solzhenitsyn was suffering in prison, the Western media had to pay him lip service, but now . . . I would really hate to see the fellow in his state of comic ignominy.

Izvestia has just sent me one of its tiresome bulletins and instructed me to include it in my upcoming book from Random House. They want me to say that minority groups in the Soviet Union "give to the nation a glow of an incipient, genuine nationalism." Now we both know that there is a great deal of information in the West about just what we do to our Armenians and Latvians. I don't want to get into this can of worms, for heaven's sake. Next they'll want me to bring up the Hitler-Stalin pact.

Sincerely yours,

Vladimir

P.S.   The economy is really on the upswing. I don't know what is going on. Could it be that the damn supply-side economics is working? We better trot out some columns about how—a) This is a Keynesian recovery, b) This is prosperity obtained at the cost of the poor, and c) This is all very short-lived.

April 1984

My dear Alex:

You would be wise not to repeat the sentiments expressed in your last letter to me regarding the research Moscow has asked you to carry out. Just because your work is being praised by *The New York Review of Books* does not mean you are too hot a property to conduct what you refer to as "mental drudgery." And, in case you have forgotten, we still have the files connecting both your parents to a number of their Jewish friends. The Party might detect just the faintest note of Hebrew superiority in your attitude.

Besides, you would, if you thought about it, be honored that Moscow has singled out you to report on the important work of the Union of Concerned Scientists (UCS). Perhaps you are not aware that their attack on Reagan's Star Wars plan has already won much acclaim back home. Apparently, Sagan and Richard Garwin, who essentially wrote it, have actually come up with several ways we might try to defeat the system that had not occurred to our own scientists. So get to know them; learn to enjoy mixing.

If you want to get back in the Party's good graces, you might also write to the CIA and the State Department under the Freedom of Information Act. They must have some backdated studies on strategic defense which would be of interest. The Party may even be impressed with your initiative.

In the future, however, I would appreciate not being troubled by your petulant requests. I have let you in on tricks of the trade that have taken me years to develop. Do not come whining to me just because you are being asked now to earn your salary. The UCS has just spent a year concocting an attack on Star Wars that our own technicians could never have developed, and they are not even paid.

Sincerely yours,

Vladimir

My dear Alex:

To illustrate both your growth and our need for continued humility, I would like to quote from a letter you wrote to me in 1982:

"The appointment of George Shultz as Secretary of State is a severe setback. It can only signal a renewed effort by the military-industrial complex to reverse its losses and seize control of Reagan's foreign policy once and for all. Haig, it's true, is an old general, but as such, was only a tool of the ruling capitalist ownership class. Shultz, by contrast, is a well-known business executive, a hardheaded exploiter of the workers and a direct representative of bourgeois thinking which the angry and fuming lackey Haig could only emulate. Shultz, a tough profiteer, threatens to bring the policy of the United States into the anti-Soviet rhetoric of Reagan, and thus raises the specter of fresh moves to expand imperialist domination into new spheres."

Doesn't it feel silly to be the author of that paragraph, Alex? As you must realize by now, these allegedly "hardheaded" businessmen often turn to mush when it comes to politics. Once they turn their thoughts from inert balance sheets or stock price columns in *The Wall Street Journal* to the flesh-and-blood business of politics and controversy, war and revolution, well, they seem to metamorphose into as many jellyfishes. I notice the chairman of Pepsico Corporation, Donald Kendall, recently launched a vigorous call to expand trade with our country on the grounds that it would help pacify our foreign policy. Other leading businessmen, even some Reagan officials, are busy lobbying on behalf of assistance for Nicaragua, Cuba, and Angola.

Yes, the more I see of capitalism, the more I like capitalists, especially men like Shultz. I know that you're a bit confused about him, because of his anti-Soviet rhetoric and his formal, public stance of always backing Reagan. Remember, though, that with someone like Shultz, it's mainly the implementation we're interested in. You're too young to remember John Foster Dulles, but he was always bristling about "rolling back" our advances and "going to the brink" with nuclear weapons. In the end, however, his policy under Eisenhower did us no damage. Reagan's rhetoric is dangerous because we know he might take some action; but fortunately, with Shultz at the State Department, that seems unlikely. Consider:

1) Our allies in Mozambique are under intense pressure from a pro-U.S. guerrilla group. Yet Shultz is asking Congress for aid, not for the guerrillas, but for our proxy government. The same situation exists in Angola. The U.S. is even Angola's largest trading partner.

2) William Casey, the director of the CIA, has won Reagan's approval for aid to the contras in Nicaragua. But Shultz has distributed the funds so ineptly that the money doesn't matter. Did you know that some of the loot apparently goes to buy condoms and other contraceptives? Hilarious. Meanwhile, the U.S. continues to recognize the legitimacy of the Sandinista government, to engage in indirect negotiations with them via the "Contadora process," and indeed, to purchase millions of dollars a year in goods from them, all part of the imperative of free trade.

3) Afghanistan, too, is regularly a part of the administration's rhetoric of the "Reagan doctrine," of supporting so-called freedom fighters. But did you know that Shultz's State Department took months just to deliver a few million dollars in medical supplies to the mujaheedin; that it advises against sending "Stinger" missiles or other devices that the rebels badly need to resist our helicopter

gunship attacks; that Afghanistan continues to enjoy "Most Favored Nation" status in its trade relationship with the United States; that while the administration is distributing pennies in help to the anti-government rebels, it shells out dollars in trade benefits to the Afghan government?

With enemies like Shultz, Alex, who needs friends?

None of this means we should lay off Shultz in public, of course. In fact, just the opposite. When confronted with clay, one shapes. When confronted with a man like Shultz, one uses pub212 pressure to mold, press, and form him into whatever we want. The trick is to keep George attacking us with words—which don't really hurt so much—but not sticks and stones.

Behind the scenes, however, we must do all we can to strengthen him, to build up his stature, increase his clout. That is why I've advised Gromyko to ask Shultz if a "special channel" can't be set up to deal on arms control. The channel, of course, is Shultz himself. This not only flatters George, it makes him more important to Reagan. If I know Gromyko, he'll give George little bits of information here and there; insist on talking to George alone about sensitive matters, and so on—anything to give George an edge in his own bureaucratic battles, to make him a more central player, to provide him with insights that others don't have, and to create both the appearance and the reality that all important talks with the Soviets take place through the Secretary of State.

Whatever you think of these tactics, though, you must stop thinking of the class of capital owners and managers as our chief enemies. Lenin was only half right when he said the Westerners would sell us the rope to hang them with, Alex. He forgot to say the rope would be subsidized—by men like George Shultz with a passionate belief in the free market.

Sincerely yours,

Vladimir

My dear Alex:

For the last few months, I have been embarking upon an intensive campaign to undermine the contras in Nicaragua and the government in El Salvador. I was somewhat reluctant to inform you of this undertaking until I could show you some tangible results:

I am very proud of several recent quotations from U.S. Congressmen:

Rep. Ron Dellums: "The Reagan administration's covert war against the government of Nicaragua is clearly illegal. It is yet another example of the cowboy mentality of the President and CIA."

Rep. Norm Mineta: "How did we get so enmeshed in the Vietnam War? The answer is that the political leadership of both parties failed this country. Let us not fail the American people again. If Congress fails to stop the President, we will share responsibility for this new, open-ended, and unnecessary war."

Rep. George Miller: "Institutionalized murder by the government of El Salvador is made possible by the dollars given by this administration with the consent of the Congress. The very survival of the oligarchy and the military corruption depends on the existence of the death squads, on political repression—and on American dollars . . . We have made El Salvador into a client state and now we are a captive of that client."

Should my Central American efforts continue to succeed, Alex, there might be a promotion in it for me down to Managua. I'll miss shopping at Bloomingdales, but I'll look forward to the warmer climate down south. These northern

American winters are beginning to resemble those in the motherland.

Sincerely yours,

Vladimir

My dear Alex:

A nasty little situation is developing in El Salvador which requires my presence. It seems the upcoming elections there may come off without any violence, major fraud, or any similar incident. I am off not so much to foment anything as to gather some facts. So you are going to have to shoulder most of the load for a few days. Alex, think of it as a test run for a much bigger effort this fall, but be cautious.

Why don't you write something hinting at the "fraud and corruption which we all know takes place in a Latin election." Here you are simply drawing on conventional wisdom. Not only are charges like this nice and vague—try to refute that, Bill Buckley, ha! ha!—but they undermine the honesty of any election down there in any country, before it takes place, and whether or not we are able to generate any concrete evidence of cheating.

Realize, however, that even this line of attack carries with it some danger. In even talking about elections, we are on the enemy's turf. If a democracy has been corrupted by cheating, then it could be fixed up by eliminating the cheating. I notice Reagan now has several programs, such as the National Endowment for Democracy, designed to help countries carry out American-style elections. You know that I have never taken these nuts and bolts seriously, but Americans do.

That is why the best work in this area is done by people like Michael Kinsley at *The New Republic*. Notice his recent TRB column on the programs mentioned. Mike's tone is especially important: See how he doesn't so much raise a bunch of objections to the idea as he does snicker at it. Indeed, the piece is so effective that he probably got some very nasty responses from the old Woodrow Wilson Democrats.

It is a sign of how far we have come that Wilson's rallying cry, "Make the world safe for democracy," is now used derisively.

Sincerely yours,

Vladimir

My dear Alex:

Things are not going so well in El Salvador. The democratic stench is everywhere. I spent several days looking for some hard evidence connecting Roberto D'Aubuisson, to the death squads, but found nothing substantial. I'm afraid there may be nothing more here than the charge in the American press that D'Aubuisson is "linked" to the killings.

All this may hold up, but I get nervous when we do not have a little more backup, even if it is a kind of bumblebee theory. One of the things you learn in this business is that over the long haul, you have to do your homework.

It is hard for me to see how to turn the race to our advantage. I kind of like the argument being promoted by *The Washington Post* to the effect that the U.S. cannot allow D'Aubuisson to be elected. This puts the *Post* in the position of saying the U.S. must consider "strong action" to make sure Napolean Duarte wins it.

This is very useful in undermining the election's legitimacy whatever happens; if D'Aubuisson wins, the military killers are running the show and the U.S. must withdraw support; if Duarte wins as the result of U.S. help, then the exercise loses moral authority, and the government is a puppet. Do you remember what happened when Kennedy ordered the removal of Diem in Vietnam? Suddenly the U.S. was culpable for every abuse that took place there.

And yet, let us consider it from the other angle. If Duarte wins, the *Post* will lose much of its rationale for attacking El Salvador's human rights abuses; it, like Reagan, will be tied to the result. This now appears likely. On the outside chance D'Aubuisson takes it—well, what happens if he has been in office for two months and there is no bloodbath? Even Duarte has been running around the country saying D'Aubuisson is not a murderer, but a good man, committed to the democratic process. If he should win despite the U.S. effort to defeat him, he might also aggressively pursue and win the war against the rebels, and our side will have to start all over again.

No, I think we are better off simply arguing, as *The New Republic* does in its latest editorial, that in some bland way, "the military runs the country anyway." Then we can get back to talking about poverty, diverting attention from democracy and putting it back on capitalism. Not only is the poverty obviously there and unarguably bad, it is likely to remain there, whatever the vicissitudes of these damn voting practices. Indeed, I am already preparing a piece to run three months or so from now, noting that "the elections, tragically, have solved nothing for the three-quarters of El Salvador's people whose income is less than $2,000 per year. Indeed, how could they? To the working peasant who struggles to survive—against hunger and the right-wing death squads— the exercise is a cruel charade, a way of legitimizing the rule of well-heeled oligarchs and powerful military elites. He needs bread, not ballots and slogans."

We, for our part, need to make sure that Marxism is up against capitalism, not democracy. It is awfully hard for a Westerner to defend his two cars and power lawnmower with the fervency with which he defends his right to elect the President of the United States—even though he probably didn't even vote last time, and even though he may care more in his heart for his comforts than for his abstract political rights. The more we can shift the discussion to lawnmowers, the more squeamish the enemy will become.

The sooner the Salvadoran elections are over, in my book, the better, and then we can all get back to talking about land reform.

Sincerely yours,

Vladimir

My dear Alex:

For once your analysis is right on the mark. I continue to read with great concern the recent critical reports by *U.S. News and World Report* correspondent Nicholas Daniloff. He has clearly violated the tacit agreement prohibiting consistent criticism of our glorious homeland. The man has terrible manners. What's more, he is quite dangerous.

While people at *The New York Times* are busy glorifying our public pronouncements promising to crack down on corruption and bureaucratic red tape, Daniloff is consistently harping on our more unpleasant qualities. His latest cover story: "Andropov: A Year of Failure," is quite damaging. Bill Dunn, in introducing the article, remarks how our KGB agents follow American reporters in Moscow and tap their phone lines and how Russian employees of Western media report their activities to the government. Besides all this, Dunn concludes, "the winters seem to last forever." Daniloff goes on to criticize Yuri's "inflexibility" and his preparation "to confront the U.S. more directly." He even went as far as saying that our system of governing "puts an entire nation in a straitjacket."

After reading this article, I had my intern look up some of Daniloff's previous writings. I was shocked. He has authored pieces with titles like "Why Russians Will Go Right on Spying," "Behind Boasts, the Grim Side of Soviet Medicine," "For Russia: Stunted Crops, Stunted Hopes," "Religion's Fight for Survival in Russia," "For Russia's Women, Worst of both Worlds," "In Russia, Squeeze on Consumer Gets Tighter," "Ahead for Andropov, Troubles on All Sides," and another damaging cover story titled "Is the Military Taking Over the Kremlin?"

We have had so many friendly writers and scholars come

out of Harvard that I have to wonder where they went wrong with this fellow Daniloff. I'm quite concerned about this rebellious criticism that prevades his writings. I am going to suggest to our superiors in Moscow that some action be taken against him. At the very least, I think they should make sure his credit card to the hard currency store be terminated. (During my stint in Moscow, I was hardly ever invited to shop there! We receive such unfair treatment.) In any event, knowing our superiors, they will probably take more serious action.

Thanks for calling this to my attention, Alex. I am pleased to see you are developing a keen eye for troublemakers.

Sincerely yours,

Vladimir

P.S.   I was happy to hear you enjoyed the Beluga cavier and Dom Perignon at the Common Cause reception. Fred sure knows how to throw a party!

My dear Alex:

I wanted to bring you up to date on some recent developments:

1. Did you catch my performance on the Donahue Show? You should see the letters I am getting. My finest moments came during the discussion of Afghanistan. When some fat lady in the audience brought up the nasty business, I equated Afghanistan with the U.S. invasion of Grenada. Then Donahue burst in to ask if I really believed the two were comparable, and I said sure. He admitted that both were brutal and unjustified, but noted that Soviet troops are still in Afghanistan. I said we were still worried about Pakistani attacks but were working on a negotiated settlement and a convenient date for a pullout, which I expected within less than a year. Donahue laughed and said he would hold me to that promise. I laughed, the audience applauded, and that was that.

2. Our comrade Georgi Arbatov has a new book out, *The Soviet Viewpoint,* which is a must. Georgi talks about his "raised consciousness." He deplores Reagan's simplistic "Us Against Them" mentality. He calls for policies based on "compromise" not "confrontation." He deplores "saber rattling" and "Cold War rhetoric." He wants "reciprocity" to alleviate "world tensions." Hardliners in the Pentagon should override their "vested interests" in the "military-industrial complex." More weight should be given to "pragmatists." After all, "We are talking about nothing less than survival of life on this planet." Besides, there are "social costs" to this massive military buildup." There is "widespread alienation" and "social

atomization." More attention should be paid to "meaningful redistribution" of income.

3. The French socialist Louis Mermaz has come up with a formulation that we would do well to memorize. Confronted with a detailed documentation of the death toll in the gulag, he righteously replied, "I am as horrified as you are by the gulags, which are a perversion of Communism. But I ask that you also condemn that monstrosity of the capitalist system: hunger throughout the world that kills 50 million people each year." Consider the outrage, Alex, if President Reagan, when asked about the problem of hunger in the world, replied with a diatribe against the gulag. Isn't it nice that we benefit from such oneway analogies?

4. Have you read the Congressmen's letter extending a friendly hand to Daniel Ortega and the Sandinistas, Alex? "Dear Commandante: We have been, and remain, opposed to U.S. support for military action directed against the people or government of Nicaragua . . . We want to commend you and the members of your government for taking steps to open up the political process in your country . . . We recognize that you have taken these steps in the midst of ongoing hostilities on the borders of Nicaragua . . . A decision on your part to provide reasonable assurances and conduct truly free and open elections would significantly improve the prospect of better relations between our two countries and significantly strengthen the hands of those in our country who desire better relations based upon true equality, self-determination and mutual goodwill. Signed, Jim Wright, Michael Barnes, Bill Alexander, Matthew McHugh, Robert Turicelli, Edward Boland, Stephen Solarz, David Obey, Robert Garcia, Lee Hamilton." Great stuff, Alex. I must say, I did not realize we had come this far with

the Democratic Party. We are seeing the American opposition directly promote our surrogates. More amazing, this sort of thing is permitted in America. Imagine Comrade Ustinov or Comrade Gorbachev conducting personal diplomacy and striking deals with sworn enemies of our country! Anywhere else, this behavior would be treason; in America, it is "broadening the channels of communication."

We should work to encourage the idea that since America is a democracy, virtually anybody can claim to speak for the nation's interests, certainly anybody elected to local office or published in a foreign affairs journal. This way we'll have Ronald Reagan, Jesse Jackson, and Tom Wicker all striking deals with foreign powers, to the delightful confusion of all, and direct advantage to us.

Congratulations on your last column on Central America in which you describe the problems there as "indigenous." All Communist activities in Third World countries should always be described as "indigenous."

5. In your last letter you asked me for arguments about why President Reagan was mistaken to declare the Middle East a region of vital strategic interest. I offer a paragraph from a recent book, *Beyond the Freeze*, by the Union of Concerned Scientists. "Rather than readying troops to fight for oil in remote deserts, the U.S. would do far better to employ a new army of construction engineers to install energy-saving technology in America's cars, homes, and factories."

Sincerely yours,

Vladimir

P.S. I just got my Jerry Falwell dartboard in the mail with a nice note from Common Cause. The people over there don't like the Ayatollah Khomeini dartboard that is selling so well all over the country, and I can see why. It fails to take into account the legitimate concerns of the Iranian mullahs over American actions in the past. But Falwell is an absolute monster who has no appreciation at all of the wall separating church and state.

My dear Alex:

"Star Wars" is shaping up nicely as a possible election issue, but I confess to a growing unease over our position. As you know, Moscow is getting more and more concerned about the whole program. My latest instructions are to make this a top priority for fall; indeed, for years to come. We're in trouble if we don't come up with something here. So I want you to put on your thinking cap; this is a long-run problem that requires some planning, and I'm thinking of a radical change in strategy.

The problem, Alex, is that the old Star-Wars-can't-work arguments don't seem to be going very far. Remember that study by the Union of Concerned Scientists you were looking into? The one that concluded an actual defense would cost trillions?

Well, it turns out the key calculation on which all this was based involved the number of satellites needed to knock down our missiles. This in turn hinges on other things, like putting the satellites into the most efficient orbits, pointing them in the right direction, and so on. That's the trouble with these "scientific studies"—they always hinge on a few key assumptions that are highly debatable and which change the whole question.

To make a long story short, the UCS—Dick Garwin, Hans Bethe, Carl Sagan, and the rest—blew it. They calculated several thousand satellites would be needed, and since the things will cost between $250 million and $1 billion each, well, it's easy to get into the trillions. But it won't take thousands of satellites, Alex. The figure has already been revised downward to several hundred by Bethe, and I hear Garwin is being pressed to admit some other errors too, bringing the estimate down to—hold your breath—about 75 satellites!

Please keep this in strictest confidence, Alex. I know all this only because Sagan is getting pummelled so badly on his nuclear winter theory that he's been pestering some of our own scientists to rush out some more studies backing him up. (Carl's right; Velikov is awfully slow. Did you check into his progress as I asked?) Anyway, the word is out that a physicist up at Dartmouth College, Robert Jastrow, has been poking into all this and may be working on a piece exposing the UCS errors for *Commentary*. That would be quite a setback.

Even setting all these errors aside, it's becoming clear that defense can work. After all, we already have a defense against American missiles and if our scientists can do it, you know the Americans can do it too. Just a couple of weeks ago, the Americans successfully shot up an unarmed missile and shot it down miles above the earth with another one guided by a sophisticated computer. These "smart missiles" are cheap, and with them our huge investment in establishing nuclear superiority is smashed.

Rather than arguing Star Wars can "never work," we should start to make grudging admissions about our "fears" of the program. Admittedly, this will tend to undercut our friends, who have held that Star Wars is an enormous boondoggle. But frankly, those groups have already done their work, creating the vague impression that defense will be very costly and risky. They've gone as far as they can go. It's now going to be up to us to show that even if some defenses can work, they will stand in the way of something far more valuable:

Arms control.

Yes, Alex, we are going to have to argue that Star Wars is such an immense threat to the strategic balance that it must be cancelled in order to get us to agree to an arms control treaty. One nice thing about this argument is that we can make it so. As long as Star Wars moves ahead, we will simply say, no deal. Soon it will be obvious that we are serious, and then our friends will be able to put the onus for the failure of arms control not on us, but on Ronald Reagan. After all, our demand that Star Wars be stopped will be well known. Hence, the only suspense will involve whether or not Reagan accepts our terms. Hence, the choice of whether or not there is ever to be an arms control treaty will seem to be—indeed will be—entirely up to him.

Fortunately, Reagan has not yet deployed any defenses. This gives us time to build up concern that such a step would be dangerous and provocative. Reagan will be forced to offer ever-more-generous reassurances that his program is meant for "research only" and won't yield defenses for "many years." This will make defense seem, as its critics argue, a thing far off in the future, a rather ethereal, hypothetical prospect— as against the concrete, immediate chance for "an agreement to pull mankind back from the brink of nuclear holocaust."

Remember, Alex, it's deployment we want to block. If Star Wars is never deployed, who cares how much money is spent researching it? So the first thing we need to do is to inculcate the right ideas about what sort of achievement, in terms of technology, would justify deployment. The standard we want to establish is that only a leakproof, totally invulnerable shield is worth having as a defense. Naturally, such a standard can never be met, not even by the Americans. Even my coffee-maker breaks down now and then. So how can a defense against thousands of nuclear weapons ever be expected to work flawlessly?

This seems to be a technical argument, I realize. But that's the beauty of it: It sounds scientific, but it really has nothing to do with science at all.

Sooner or later some Star Wars test will fail, or a missile will misfire—who knows, maybe that damn space shuttle will blow up—and then it will be time to remind everyone "how futile it is to rely on a technological fix to solve our political problems." At last, we will be on solid ground. Indeed, the more money spent on mere research, the more it will seem that the quest for perfect defense is ridiculous. By the time Reagan, or some successor, is ready to construct a real defense, we and our friends will have spent years building up the idea that only a perfect shield will do. Think of the outrage, the shock, the disappointment we can all then express when some President proposes to actually do something about Star Wars.

                         Sincerely yours,

                         Vladimir

My dear Alex:

The reason for this note is to draw your attention to David Ansen's obituary of Lillian Hellman in the latest *Newsweek*. I have always liked Dave, but this time he surpassed himself. "The Hellman anger arose from her clear-eyed view of social injustice and strong moral convictions, and she remained true to her passion throughout her rich and tumultuous life. Not for her the modernist halftones of alienation and equivocation. The fire within her lit up the cultural landscape; its heat will be deeply missed." This is Ansen's way of saying that Hellman was sympathetic to the Soviet Union. She was not part of the liberal anti-Communist consensus that encompassed Lionel Trilling and Mary McCarthy. Hellman was one of ours.

Today fellow travelling has gone out of vogue, however, so Ansen discreetly skipped over Hellman's more sycophantic comments about Stalin. Apparently the only criticism she could make of the Great Comrade was that his policies constituted "infringements on personal liberty."

If you read Hellman's work, Alex, you will see how effectively culture can be manipulated to our ends. In her 1976 book, *Scoundrel Time*, for instance, Hellman chronicles her life in the American gulag, a subtle kind of prison, perhaps, but a prison made all the more insidious by its absence of bars, wardens, and hard labor. This sort of hyperbole is quite acceptable in the literary milieu, and yet it erodes the ability of the American intelligentsia to make sharp distinctions between the U.S. and our country. The Hollywood purges become morally equivalent to Stalin's purges. Great stuff.

I hope this helps persuade you that American culture is not the "worthless decadence" you insist on calling it. American intellectuals are thoroughly alienated from their own society and harbor the strongest prejudices against representative democracy and bourgeois capitalism—neither of which assign great importance to intellectuals over the common people. We can accommodate this alienation to serve our interests. But—like Ansen—we have to be subtle.

Sincerely yours,

Vladimir

My dear Alex:

Remember President Reagan's speech after the KAL shooting in which he called the Soviet Union's actions a "crime against humanity"? How far we have come since then! With most of the American people the incident is largely forgotten, and now I am told that the American journalist Seymour Hersh is writing a book on the subject.

I have not yet seen the Hersh manuscript—my friends at the publishing house are being tightfisted with the copy—but, my dear Alex, when we are dealing with Hersh we have nothing to worry about. Here is a man truly committed to the cause of anti-Americanism. In other words, he is a man after my own heart.

Hersh has built his reputation on undermining the confidence of the American people in their government. From Vietnam to Watergate, he has exposed the lies and corruption that are at the core of American democracy. Perhaps you suspect that, having done this, he will now turn his sights to the Soviet Union. But never fear. That is not the way things work.

Even without seeing the Hersh manuscript, I feel confident that he will find some way to blame the Reagan administration and exonerate us for what we did. Perhaps he will be able to cook the evidence to show that the Korean airliner was a spy plane. Perhaps he won't have evidence, but will just kick up such a cloud of smoke and ambiguity that will leave a confused memory in the public mind. (This is damage control.) Alternatively, Hersh may put the whole thing down to aviation error but nevertheless fault the Reagan administration for bellicose rhetoric, provoking the Soviet Union, heightening tensions, bringing us closer to World War III—you know the litany.

Let's put in an advance order for a few hundred books. There is still some bitterness at the Kremlin over this KAL incident. I am sure that Hersh's book will go a long way to lifting morale. Needless to add, this will be good for you and me in the long-run.

Sincerely yours,

Vladimir

My dear Alex:

Jeane Kirkpatrick's likely departure from her post as U.S. Ambassador to the United Nations is the best news I have heard in quite a while.

Many things depressed me about Kirkpatrick, not least her liberal Democratic background. This woman used to be a disciple of Hubert Humphrey, no less. Granted, Humphrey is not treated kindly in some of our textbooks back home, Alex, but the man was pretty effective at the margin in undercutting U.S. defense policy. Besides, he evolved from someone quite hawkish to someone quite conciliatory. My friends in the American media refer to this process of becoming more appeasement-oriented as "growing."

The larger problem with Kirkpatrick, though, is the intellectual scaffolding that she has helped build for right-wing foreign policy doctrine. Previously, such doctrine was guided only by a general animus toward the Soviet Union. Being unfocused and largely emotional, it could be scoffed at. But Kirkpatrick has given redneck emotion a rationale—a case that, to most Americans, would be very convincing.

I have still not fully recovered from Kirkpatrick's 1979 *Commentary* essay, "Dictatorships and Double Standards," in which she argued that traditional dictatorships can evolve into liberal, Western-style democracies, while Communist regimes never do.

We can be thankful that there were many in the administration and in the Democratic Party who immediately set out to destroy Kirkpatrick. The American left is especially well-disposed to Third World Communism. This is all to the good.

Unfortunately, no one seems to have been able to punch holes in Kirkpatrick's thesis. Efforts to dismiss it altogether were not successful. *Mother Jones* and the old-reliable press tried to defend the human rights records of countries in the socialist fraternity but this (as I noted in a conversation with one of the editors) was a strategy destined to fail from the start. Finally, at my belated suggestion, a campaign was launched to suggest that Kirkpatrick was doing all this to justify and coddle rightist dictatorships—that somehow she approved of torture and rapine as long as it was done by a well-groomed dictator, and not by a Communist in battle fatigues. This strategy got further than the previous ones, but ultimately it, too, did not do the job.

Now Kirkpatrick is going and the administration has lost one of its stronger voices. Naturally we still have to fear what she will do in private life. But I am not too worried. Kirkpatrick will be absorbed in the money-chase of capitalism. She will give $20,000 speeches before trade associations and Rotary Clubs. She will take trips abroad. She will do lots of newspaper interviews. Success, in other words, will neutralize her. She will evangelize her ideas to lots of people, but most likely they will forget what she said in a few days. There will be no incentive for her to produce any more of the kind of scholarship that made her famous.

Sincerely yours,

Vladimir

My dear Alex:

I am really getting mad at *The New York Times*. Did you see Claire Sterling's June 10 article linking the Bulgarians to the attempt to kill the Pope? All that summation of evidence in one place—it's bad. I just don't understand it: The *Times* has repeatedly editorialized on our behalf; you remember the stuff they did on Grenada. But now this. I tell you, Alex, we may be seeing one of our most useful propaganda organs reverting to its previous bad form. This is serious.

The *Times* used to be an enemy of Soviet objectives. In 1956, they editorialized against our liberation of Hungary by noting, "We accuse the Soviet government of murder. We accuse it of the basest deceit known to man. We accuse it of having committed so monstrous a crime against the Hungarian people that its infamy can never be forgotten or forgiven." But a few years later, by the time we went into Czechoslovakia, they had forgotten. The Great Scribe Tony Lewis noted that "The West can help most by remaining quiet and calm." The *Times* blamed our intervention on "the failure of U.S. diplomacy."

Then came Vietnam and Watergate. Writers at the *Times* became openly hostile to the U.S. government and American institutions. No longer were Americans viewed as the "good guys." Thus the struggle with our country was seen as purely opportunistic—two imperialists with their horns locked. The *Times* became superciliously neutral in the struggle between East and West, though in fact it helped our side because its attacks on our leaders had absolutely no effect, while it effectively undermined faith in the U.S. system of government, not to speak of getting rid of several politicians who opposed appeasement.

Until now, I have been rather pleased with The *Times'*

coverage of Central America. The paper has focused on human rights violations in El Salvador while virtually ignoring the situation in Nicaragua. I feel particularly affectionate toward Alan Riding for his wonderful pieces on literacy in Nicaragua. He even makes excuses for the Nicaraguans not holding elections. Warren Hoge, another writer I have come to like, noted in January 1982 that "It is indisputable that Nicaraguans today suffer less state repression of fundamental freedoms than do the people of countries in the region like Guatemala and El Salvador whose right-wing governments do not draw the same kind of critical commentary from Washington." With enemies like these, Alex, who need friends?

The Sterling article has alerted me to a possible change of mood at the *Times*, however. I have also been noticing the anti-Communist articles appearing in the Sunday *Magazine*, which has recently been brought under the control of executive director Abraham Rosenthal. We kicked that bastard out of Poland because he was sticking it to Gomulka and our other boys there. But perhaps we were too aggressive with Rosenthal, because now he is in a position to greatly inconvenience us. Damn. All the Western journalists want is to be well fed, and permitted to travel around and interview a few people with different points of view from the government. Give them that, and they will accept the basic legitimacy of our system in a moment.

Sincerely yours,

Vladimir

September 1984

My dear Alex:

The inside word from the Kremlin is that Chernenko is ailing now and soon we may have a new leader. The rumor is that it could be the suave Mikhail Gorbachev. For myself, I hope he does come to power. I was personally unknown to Andropov and Chernenko before they rose to the top, but Gorbachev I know pretty well. We were fellow Stalinists in the old days, and worked together on some ingenious fabrications of evidence that ultimately led to a whole bunch of forced confessions. He's ruthless, but with a sense of humor. Would you believe that through all the painful show trials he not only kept a straight face but smiled from ear to ear? Wish I could do that. Master of theatrical skills and strategy though I am, I don't think I could ever rival him.

Successions are always a complicated business, Alex. This letter is to prepare you for the kind of approach you should take to help legitimize the current Soviet leader with the American press and public. The general idea, which you should have surmised from my reports on Andropov and Chernenko, is that the new man is a "reformer." The new man, whoever he is, whatever his background, should be presented as a sharp break with the reactionary Soviet politics of the past. Hints should be dropped about economic decentralization, crackdowns on corruption, taste for Western music (I was particularly effective on this last count with Andropov), etc.

Now, you may wonder how we can get away with it time after time? We say Andropov is a reformer and he turns out to be an old KGB type. We make the same claims about Chernenko, who hardly looks the part of a blazing reformer, and he too turns out to be an old school Marxist. Aren't people going to see that this is a ridiculous and implausible game we are playing, trying to build faith in the new leader on predictably specious grounds?

Alex, Alex, if you were convinced by this last paragraph, I am afraid you still do not understand America very well. Let me just give you some samples of published materials in the Western press—from journalists, even from Soviet specialists—which suggest how gullible and malleable these people are.

LENIN

WALTER DURANTY, *The New York Times*, October 6, 1921.
[Lenin has a] cool, far sighted, reasoned sense of realities . . . [He is willing to] put aside what experience has shown to be impracticable theories and devote himself to rebuilding Russia on a new and solid foundation.

STEPHEN COHEN, *Bukharin and the Bolshevik Revolution* (New York, 1973).
(Lenin's) New Economic Policy, like Weimar culture, was a major chapter in the cultural history of the 20th century, one that created brilliantly, died tragically, but left an enduring influence . . .
It was this toleration of social diversity, as well as the official emphasis on social harmony and the rule of law, as opposed to official lawlessness, that 30 years later would commend the N.E.P. to Communist Party reformers as a model of a liberal Communist order, an alternative to Stalinism.

STALIN

LOUIS FISCHER, *The Nation*, March 19, 1930.
One returns to the country to find not only new achievements, radically new policies, and new social atmosphere, but a powerful, all enveloping, newly released wave or wall of energy and enthusiasm . . .
Everything moves here. Life, the air, people are dynamic. When I watch these recently unsealed reservoirs of energy I

am sometimes carried away and think that nothing is impossible in the Soviet Union.

MALCOLM COWLEY, *The New Republic*, September 11, 1935.
[The Soviet leaders are] turning their attention to minor products—flower beds, jazz bands, joy, light wines, and the secret ballot.

W.E.B. DUBOIS, *The Seventh Son* (1937).
He [Stalin] asked for neither adulation nor vengeance. He was reasonable and conciliatory.

ANDROPOV

STEPHEN COHEN, *The Nation*, December 18, 1982.
And yet, Andropov seems to have been the most reform-minded senior member of Brezhnev's Politburo, an impression he chose to reinforce cautiously in his first policy speech as the new General Secretary. Nor does his 15-year stint as head of the K.G.B. disqualify him as a potential reformer. Soviet police chiefs, who must understand the limits of control, have become advocates of liberalizing change before. Indeed, Andropov may be the only current leader who can assuage conservative fears of reform. And lest we forget that politicians sometimes rise above their former careers, Khrushchev once was called the "Butcher of the Ukraine" for his part in Stalin's terror.

JOHN F. BURNS, *The New York Times*, November 20, 1982.
The diplomats predict that if Mr. Andropov has his way, which is far from certain, the first months of his tenure could see the beginning of a major crackdown on corruption, a cutback on some aspects of the bureaucratic red tape that entangles the Soviet system, and perhaps a move toward a slightly less rigid economic system.

DUSKO DODER, *The Washington Post*, November 20, 1982.
From what little is known about him, the somewhat professorial-looking Andropov has been better prepared for supreme

office than any of his predecessors. With the exception of Lenin, the founder of the Soviet state, he is the first intellectual in this post.

He likes theater and the arts and has written extensively on ideological matters. The 15 years he spent as head of the K.G.B. have made him probably the most informed man in the country. In that post he was, in a way, both foreign and interior minister in charge of a vast organization with foreign and domestic responsibilities.

CHERNENKO

JOHN F. BURNS *The New York Times*, February 19, 1984.
Others [i.e. diplomats] caution against underestimating Mr. Chernenko, who impressed several Western leaders who met him after the funeral as a warmer, earthier man than Mr. Andropov, seemingly comfortable in his new role. Like Deng Xiaoping, who capped an even more remarkable comeback in China by launching radical reforms, Mr. Chernenko could still prove to be an old man in a hurry. If so, he will confound not only his critics but still more so those in the bureaucracy who look to him for a return to the less challenging times under Mr. Brezhnev.

Chernenko is not one to delegate important decisions. But before making them himself, the source says, Chernenko encourages discussion. During these discussions, the Soviet associate says, he is open to all opinions. Once the decision is made, however, he says Chernenko will not stand for recrimination or second guessing. He is, the source adds, "a firm advocate of collective leadership," seeking consensus—but fully expecting support from everyone once the decision is made.

JERRY HOUGH, "Soviet Succession," in *Problems of Communism*, November 1982.
If Chernenko is purely a transitional leader, his policy pref-

erences might not be very important. Nevertheless, if he does become the General Secretary, the coalition he has put together and the content of speeches and articles suggest that he is a strong supporter of detente and of some kinds of reform. When Brezhnev presented Chernenko with awards on his 70th birthday, he praised his assistant for being 'restless' in the good sense of the term, a man with "a creative, daring approach." In response, Chernenko acknowledged that he sometimes makes "nonstandard decisions." He has written often of the need for "further perfection of the political system" and frequently expresses what sound like anti-bureaucratic, and proparticipatory views.

Pardon these somewhat windy quotations, Alex, but I think I have made my point. Can you imagine how crazy these fools will be about Gorbachev, who is a younger and somewhat more dapper fellow than the current crowd? I have particular hopes for his wife, Raisa—I think she can be billed as the Libby Dole of the Soviet Union. She will make an incredible impact, and will contrast favorably with the wives of Brezhnev, Andropov, and Chernenko. What dogs! (Alex, you must keep these personal asides of mine to yourself.)

Sincerely yours,

Vladimir

My dear Alex:

Ronald Reagan continues to lead in the polls, but the left is wise to force him to posture on arms control. I don't know if we handled this one correctly—by meeting with Reagan, Gromyko obviously helps his peacemaker image—and yet I cannot help but think the Politburo is reconciled to a second Reagan term, and is hoping to placate the President.

The fact that Reagan is trying to pose as a champion of detente, a President of arms control, shows the success of our strategy of the past three decades. Basically, we have been promoting as the cardinal rule of American foreign policy: "Keep talking." Implicit in this idea is the assumption that differences between the U.S. and our country can be resolved by a negotiated settlement.

We know this is not the case, but we weaken Ronald Reagan's hand if his people hold him to this belief. Everything can be solved, the West should be taught, if all countries "engage in dialogue," "try to understand each other," and "sit down and talk."

This "keep talking" rule deprives the West of flexibility and initiative in choosing when to talk and when not to talk, and on what conditions and for what purposes they are to talk. Meanwhile, our country is not obliged to "keep talking." America is thus held hostage to our interests and dependent on our approval. The success of American foreign policy is judged not by the overthrow of Communism, but by the number of agreements signed, the number of talks and dialogues conducted. Then all we have to do is only talk to the U.S. when it makes massive concessions to us.

Sincerely yours,

Vladimir

My dear Alex:

You are disturbed, I know, at the pre-election rhetoric of the Mondale-Ferraro camp. Although by now I am sure you understand that it is mere posturing, nevertheless you wonder whether they can express hostile feelings toward the motherland "without meaning it." This concern is not yours alone. I have been getting memos from the people back home wanting to know what the hell is going on.

For them I have prepared a little chart which I like to call my "Gorbachev rating." It is very similar to the various ratings the Americans prepare—you know, ratings by the Conservative Union, the Americans for Democratic Action, Christian Voice, and so on. Only my little chart traces the degree to which liberal foreign and defense policy is in concert with state Soviet policy. I have used Tip O'Neill as a spokesman for the liberal position, and Reagan for the conservative position. Here is what I came up with:

Issue	Reagan	O'Neill	Gorbachev
Pershing deployment	YES	NO	NO
Cruise-missile deployment	YES	NO	NO
Neutron bomb	YES	NO	NO
Aid to contras	YES	NO	NO
Grenada intervention	YES	NO	NO
Lifting grain embargo	YES	NO	YES
Strategic defense	YES	NO	NO

Nuclear freeze	NO	YES	YES	.
Aid to Angolan rebels	YES	NO	NO
Aid to Marxist Mozambique	YES	YES	YES
MX missile	YES	NO	NO
Disinvestment from South Africa	NO	YES	YES
Trade sanctions against Soviets	YES	NO	NO
Sanctions against Nicaragua	YES	NO	NO
Military aid to El Salvador	YES	NO	NO
Aid to Afghan rebels	YES	YES	NO

I too am getting a little tired of the anti-Soviet windbaggery on the part of the liberal Democrats, Alex, but I also realize how little practical significance it has. And believe me, after the election they are all going to be embarrassed when I remind them of the levels to which they stooped.

Democracy, Alex. It can be a real pain.

Sincerely yours,

Vladimir

My dear Alex:

I know it's frustrating that some elements of the press have begun to notice the rapid conversion of Nicaragua into an efficient, well-run base for our advance. I had already seen Robert Leiken's piece in *The New Republic* when your plaintive letter arrived. I am also fully aware that *The New York Times* has been getting worse and worse on this ever since Ray Bonner left Central America and the focus shifted from Salvadoran death squads to Sandinista "corruption and violence," as Leiken puts it.

But frankly, dealing with such unpleasant facts is our task. If our cause weren't advancing, it would be easy to placate the Americans. If everyone in the U.S. were an Alexander Cockburn, we would be out of a job. Our job is to get a few people to maintain the old line that Nicaragua is a paradise; a few others to admit that while it's no paradise, the harsh conditions there are mainly a result of the U.S.-sponsored war; a few others to say that while the place stinks, and the U.S. is hardly to blame for this, it would be "rash and counterproductive" to abandon the "Contadora process"; and still others to admit that the peace talks are a sham—but insist that the United States has no right to violate international law by conducting provocative military exercises in the region.

The longer I am in this business, the more I realize that there are a few clear, obvious victories. Our job is to keep things muddled and confused enough that nobody really wakes up to our advance—until it is too late.

Therefore, I can't agree with you that Daniel Ortega, the current Sandinista ruler, is "behaving stupidly" and "undermining our efforts" by asking for more arms, cracking down on the Catholic Church, and censoring *La Prensa*. In case you have forgotten, Alex, Ortega is a revolutionary. His job is to consolidate power, crush the contra resistance, and spread our influence into the rest of Latin America, ultimately to Mexico. He's going to have to step on a few toes to do that, and he's going to need plenty of guns and helicopters and jets from our government. Ortega is not, as you claim, "a dupe" merely because he does a few things that make it uncomfortable for American journalists and politicians to support his growing might. He would, on the contrary, be foolish if he behaved as you expect him to—tailoring his actions to votes on paltry amounts of contra aid in the U.S. Congress, for example.

Some of your points, I admit, are well taken. It was unnecessary for Tomas Borge to tell a major U.S. magazine, as he did recently, that "one historical prophesy of Ronald Reagan's is absolutely true," i.e., that El Salvador, Honduras, Guatemala, and Mexico are dominoes that are likely to follow the fall of Nicaragua to our forces. And it was silly of Bayardo Arce, one of the Sandinista commandantes, to comment, "We should think now about doing away with all this fiction of pluralism." No one should ever do away with the fiction of pluralism; it's the reality of pluralism that must be abolished. That's why I much prefer the argument Ortega himself made at Jackson Browne's party a few months ago: "Democracy is literacy, democracy is land reform, democracy is education and public health." By the time he got to the words "land reform," I thought Elizabeth Montgomery, Ed Asner, and Chris Dodd were going to cry. (You really have to get out to Hollywood sometime, Alex. I know they're making a few more bad films these days, but there are still plenty of good parties with our kind of people.)

The fact is, Ortega must crack down at home and get support from us to continue the revolution. Some writers in America are going to notice. Our job is to minimize the impact of this in terms of U.S. policy. The very fact that Ortega will have to keep getting rougher suggests to me our best line of explanation: We should say that his government is filled with "bunglers" and "dolts" who mean well but don't really know what they are doing, and who have been frightened into taking drastic measures because of the bloodthirsty contras.

This line should keep us in business for another couple of years, until we have several thousand more tanks in Nicaragua. At that point, it will it will appear that Danny boy has been pretty smart all along.

Sincerely yours,

Vladimir

My dear Alex:

I noticed a bit of confusion on your part the other day when that reporter asked you, "Just what is your government trying to signal in walking out of the nuclear arms reduction talks?" Alex, I thought by now you had mastered the basics. What we are always signaling, whatever we are doing, is "an interest in engaging in serious dialog for world peace." When we began deploying more submarine missiles off the American coast, for example, Tom Wicker suggested it "just might be Moscow's way" of saying we would really like to get an arms treaty, but are unsettled by the Reagan buildup in Europe. By the same token, when we walk out of an arms negotiation, we are "simply leaving a charade" in the sincere hope that it will convince Americans to submit a serious proposal. Whatever we do, we are always furthering the cause of peace.

When Castro announced that he will jam American radio broadcasts to his country, for example, many in the U.S. took it as a sign of hostility. But *The Nation* spoke for most of the left when it said "Castro is sending signals of a different sort in the other direction. He has consoled friendly governments and movements in the region to pursue cautious and accommodating policies toward Washington. He has brought back Cubans from Nicaragua, and despite the massive anti-Cuban campaign, of which the Grenada invasion was the centerpiece, he has repeatedly called for improved relations with the United States." You see? If we're friendly, it means we're friendly; if we're unfriendly, it means we're friendly.

Indeed, I sometimes muse just how we might possibly "signal" someone like Tony Lewis our intentions to start a war. I wonder if there is really anything we could do that Tony would interpret as a sign that we are out to get the U.S. Nothing comes to mind short of an invasion of Florida, and I think that would leave Alex Cockburn and some of the Arabists swearing that our motives were benign.

Anyway, I hope this clears up the confusion.

Sincerely yours,

Vladimir

My dear Alex:

I was glad to see you enter the pre-election debate on religion and politics. Glad—until I chanced upon your strident exchange with Jerry Falwell on the evening news.

Why on earth did you spend at least a third of your time defending the notion that there is freedom of religion in the Soviet Union? This is an approach that merits perhaps a passing mention, a quotation from Billy Graham or two. But no more.

The most serious problem with your presentation was the long and detailed treatise on the horrors caused by religion throughout history. I know I asked you to quote Westerners, but I did not have in mind Shelley's line to the effect that religion consists of "putrid heaps of lies." This stuff is very alienating to most people in America. I've told you before that the last thing we want to do is to clarify choices and make concrete statements and arguments, even about institutions such as the Christian church which have been largely discarded by the intellectual elite.

Mind you, I agree with your points. *Of course* the church is a dangerous roadblock to the progress of the revolution. *Of course* this Pope is a threat to world Communism. *Of course* Jerry Falwell is a reincarnation of Hitler. I say all this clearly and explicitly because I do not want you sending any more backchannel complaints to the KGB that I am beginning to harbor counter-revolutionary sentiments. Your attempt to undermine me by leaking my comments about the merits of free elections was truly shocking, and would have provoked sterner action from me if I did not have some compassion for your age and ignorance. Therefore, let us understand clearly that religion is a danger and must eventually be crushed by world socialism—when the time is right.

But in the meantime, as Lenin said, there must be backward and forward steps. There are questions of application.

You should challenge statements by Falwell and others that there are certain universal truths, not by arguing that the church is evil, but that there is no evil, and that the church is dangerous, running counter to pluralism, free expression, and free choice.

The usual response of the clergyman will be, yes, pluralism and free choice are fine, but that people must be free to choose religion as well. If Falwell had made this argument you could have come back with:

"Reverend Falwell makes a convincing argument that religion, like sexual preference is a personal choice, and one to be tolerated in a free, open society. No one is against religion in that sense. But there are a couple of troubling aspects. For one, Falwell himself is not tolerant when it comes to a woman's choice to control her own body." (All this namby-pamby argument on abortion will tire you, Alex, but some people here take the issue seriously.)

This argument about "imposing one's morality" is very effective. We must use it relentlessly. Remember that most Americans are religious, and likely to remain so for some time. But if we can confine their religion to a tightly drawn circle, and then make that circle smaller and smaller, we can render religion as weak as if we were to hurl the churches into the sea.

Sincerely yours,

Vladimir

P.S. Alex, I am just about to mail this when news about that clumsy fool Farrakhan comes to me. Was that you I saw on local TV praising him as "a visionary critic of American decadence?" Did my ears serve me correctly that you are planning to deliver a speech "Farrakhan: Monster or Man Ahead of His Time?" to the B'nai B'rith group in New York? Don't you ever learn, Alex? Or do you just have terrible relapses? Stop. Before it's too late. Farrakhan is a menace. I know you like him because he seems to embody all the contradictions of the American left. But that is precisely why I think he should be silenced. The man is blowing the whistle on our friends.

My dear Alex:

Reagan has been reelected. I must say, the news did not come to me as a shock. It was becoming pretty clear that we were going to have to put up with four more years of this man. I do not think, frankly, that even our best efforts could have prevented this debacle. After all, the Democratic Party picked terrible candidates. The media didn't help us much either—Reagan simply went over their heads to the American people. Jesse Jackson, on whom we placed such hopes, turned out to be a net minus.

It would be absurd to view Reagan's reelection as a victory for us, and yet it is not the end of the world. One has to develop a long term perspective on these things. Between 1974 and 1979, you will remember, Alex, nine countries fell to Communist control: South Vietnam, Laos, Cambodia, Afghanistan, Ethiopia, Angola, Mozambique, Nicaragua, and Grenada. Since Reagan came to power in 1980 we have lost one pawn—Grenada—from the board. But Reagan has not seriously overturned our strategic advantage, and if our final drive has to be postponed another four years—while we ride out a second Reagan term—so be it. I do not foresee any more losses for us in the next 48 months.

And yet, Alex, our superiors are not men of nuance. They do not take the same broad view of the recent elections as I do. To put it bluntly, they are furious, and they want blood.

They need me, Alex. They won't admit as much, but they do. I am American born, American educated. Sometimes I don't play by their rules, but they know that I can play the game as well as anyone they have got. This time I did not deliver, but then I have given them a reason.

The reason, Alex, is you. You screwed up. You made quite a bit of progress by the end, but it was too late. You were not sent here to help decide the outcome of the 1996 elections. You had to learn fast, but you didn't. As a result, you made blunders that advanced our enemy. You embarrassed many valuable people on our side. You blew the cover off at least five sympathizers who were previously regarded with reverence by the American left. Finally, you made it so that a great deal of my valuable time was spent instructing you on basic strategies that you should have picked up on your own.

Even if my suspicion is true, Alex, that we could not have stopped Reagan's second term, nevertheless I hold you responsible for the defense improvements of the first Reagan term, particularly strategic defense, which will cause our people headaches for the next several decades.

That is why I fully approve of the decision regarding your future, while feeling a bit sorry for you. Where you are headed it tends to get rather cold, even in the summer. I can't say I'd like to be in your place, Alex, but I hear it is bearable if you take the attitude that suffering is redemptive for the soul. At least remember to take lots of blankets.

This is a rather hurried goodbye. I shall probably not see you again. You did not help my situation here, comrade, but if there is anything I can do for your wife and infant son, I will consider it.

> *Sincerely yours,*
>
> Vladimir

DINESH D'SOUZA is the managing editor of *Policy Review*, the flagship journal of The Heritage Foundation. He writes frequently on politics for *The New York Times*, *The Washington Post*, *The Boston Globe*, *Harper's*, *Vanity Fair*, and other publications. He is author of *Before the Millennium* (Regnery Gateway, 1984) and *The Catholic Classics* (Our Sunday Visitor, 1986). He graduated Phi Beta Kappa from Dartmouth College in 1983 where he was editor of *The Dartmouth Review*.

GREGORY FOSSEDAL is a media fellow at the Hoover Institution, a contributing editor of *Harper's*, and former editorial writer at *The Wall Street Journal*. He writes frequently on politics for *Commentary*, *The New Republic*, *Reader's Digest*, and other publications. He is co-author, with General Daniel Graham, of *A Defense that Defends* (Devin Adair, 1984). He graduated Phi Beta Kappa from Dartmouth College in 1981 where he was a founder of *The Dartmouth Review*.